# PATTON
## AND THE BATTLE OF THE BULGE

Michael and Gladys Green

MBI Publishing Company

*To our good friends Ron and Joan Hare, for all their help and support during the completion of this book and many others.*

First published in 1999 by MBI Publishing Company, 729 Prospect Avenue, PO Box 1, Osceola, WI 54020-0001 USA

© Michael Green, 1999

All rights reserved. With the exception of quoting brief passages for the purpose of review no part of this publication may be reproduced without prior written permission from the Publisher.

The information in this book is true and complete to the best of our knowledge. All recommendations are made without any guarantee on the part of the author or Publisher, who also disclaim any liability incurred in connection with the use of this data or specific details.

We recognize that some words, model names and designations, for example, mentioned herein are the property of the trademark holder. We use them for identification purposes only. This is not an official publication.

MBI Publishing Company books are also available at discounts in bulk quantity for industrial or sales-promotional use. For details write to Special Sales Manager at Motorbooks International Wholesalers & Distributors, 729 Prospect Avenue, PO Box 1, Osceola, WI 54020-0001 USA.

Library of Congress Cataloging-in-Publication Data
Green, Michael.
   Patton and the Battle of the Bulge/Michael Green & Gladys Green.
      p. cm.
   Includes index.
   ISBN 0-7603-0652-4
   1. Ardennes, Battle of the, 1944–1945. 2. Patton, George S. (George Smith), 1885–1945—Military leadership. I. Green, Gladys. II. Title.
D756.5.A7G7          1999
940.54'21431—dc21      99-22933

**On the front cover:** This rare color photo of American M4 Sherman medium tanks in the Ardennes depicts a scene that was typical for Patton's forces during the Battle of the Bulge. Difficult, snowy conditions and dense forests were obstacles both sides had to overcome. *Author collection*

**On the back cover, top:** On January 4 the Germans launched another series of attacks around Bastogne that managed to blunt the advance of Patton's Third Army. As the two sides struggled in the fierce Ardennes winter, neither Patton nor his troops could see any end to the bloody fighting. *U.S. Army Photo*

**On the back cover, bottom:** The German XLVII Panzer Corps commander became worried about a relief column from Patton's III Corps pushing through his lines into Bastogne on the evening of Christmas Day. He requested additional reinforcements and wanted to call off the attacks on Bastogne. The German Fifth Army had no more reinforcement to commit. Pictured reviewing a map together are Patton and Major General Troy H. Middleton commander of Patton's VIII Corps during the fighting in the Ardennes. *Patton Museum*

Designed by Bruce Leckie

Printed in the United States of America

# Contents

|  | Acknowledgments | 4 |
|---|---|---|
|  | Introduction | 5 |
| Chapter One | Opening Moves | 6 |
| Chapter Two | The German Attack and American Reaction | 40 |
| Chapter Three | The Road to Bastogne | 82 |
| Chapter Four | Clearing the Bastogne Area | 116 |
|  | Index | 159 |

# Acknowledgments

Special thanks are due to the National Archives, Patton Museum of Cavalry and Armor, the British Army Tank Museum, and the George S. Patton, Jr., Historical Society, whose support and help made this book possible. Thanks are also due to the U.S. Army Armor School Library at Fort Knox, Kentucky, and the 4th and 5th Armored Division Associations. George Hoffman of the 6th Armored Division Association was kind enough to allow us to use pictures from his division's files. Individuals who made an extra effort in helping include Charles Lemons (Patton Museum curator), Fred Pernell (Assistant Branch Chief, Reference Still Picture Branch, National Archives), Judy Stephenson (Armor School Librarian), David Fletcher (British Army Tank Museum Curator), and Charles Province (President and Founder of the Patton Historical Society). Other friends who offered their kind assistance include Jacques Littlefield, Linda Brubaker, Dennis Riva, Ray Denkhaus, Milton Hasley, Jr., Dick Hunnicutt, Frank Schulz, Andreas Kirchhoff, Richard Byrd, Richard Cox, George Bradford, Mert Wreford, Richard Pemberton, and Karl and Carol Vonder Linden.

**Note To The Reader**

Those who wish to learn more about Patton and his Third Army, or the Battle of the Bulge, will find a list of excellent books in the selected bibliography. Unfortunately, many of the books listed are long out of print. Copies may be found at public libraries, or they can be purchased through used book dealers who specialize in military titles.

Another valuable source of information on Patton is the George S. Patton, Jr., Historical Society. The society publishes a semiannual newsletter devoted to the study of the man. The society can be reached by writing to 3116 Thorn Street, San Diego, California 92104-4618. The society's web site is at http://members.aol.com/PattonGHQ/homeghq.html

A visit to the world-famous Patton Museum of Cavalry and Armor at Fort Knox, Kentucky, allows the viewing of various Patton artifacts, as well as the weapons and equipment employed by both the Third Army and the Germans during World War II. Information on museum hours of operation and how to visit the museum can be obtained by writing to Building 4554, Fort Knox, Kentucky 40121-0208. The museum's web site is at http://147.238.100.101/museum/.

# INTRODUCTION

The powerful German counteroffensive operation code-named "Wacht am Rhein" (Watch on the Rhine) launched against the American First Army in the early morning hours of December 16, 1944, would result in the greatest single extended land battle of World War II. To most Americans, the fierce series of battles fought in the Ardennes Forest of Belgium and Luxembourg from December 1944 through January 1945 is better known as the "Battle of the Bulge." Almost one million soldiers would eventually take part in the fighting. At its high point, the German offensive operation would create a crescent-shaped "bulge," 60 miles deep by 80 miles wide, behind American lines.

British Prime Minister Winston Churchill would state in the House of Commons on January 18, 1945, that the Battle of the Bulge was "undoubtedly the greatest American battle of the war, and will, I believe, be regarded as an ever-famous American victory." An important player in that victory was General George S. Patton, with his Third Army.

The Battle of the Bulge was not appropriately named, because it consisted of numerous battles spread over a fairly wide area at different times. The battle officially ended on January 28, 1945. On that date, the Allies had pushed the Germans back to their original December 16 starting point. The price paid by the Allied forces was terribly high. The Allies lost nearly 80,000 men to all causes, and all but 1,400 were Americans. Estimates of German casualties range from 90,000 to 120,000.

This book is not intended to be yet another history of the Battle of the Bulge. Rather, the authors will concentrate on describing, in text and pictures, the role of Patton and his Third Army in that famous struggle, and especially the 4th and 6th Armored Divisions, which played such a crucial role. To place Patton and the Third Army in the proper context of the Battle of the Bulge and provide the reader a general timeline, we will cover the period leading up to the event.

## Chapter One

# Opening Moves

Many historians and writers have suspected that the idea for the German Ardennes counteroffensive of December 16, 1944, (known to Americans as the Battle of the Bulge) was first conceived in Adolf Hitler's mind sometime during the last two weeks of July 1944. Members of his immediate headquarters staff got a glimpse of the idea during a meeting on July 31, 1944.

The first official pronouncement by Hitler on his intention to mount a decisive attack on the western front occurred at his East Prussian headquarters (nicknamed the Wolf's Lair) during a meeting on Saturday, September 16, 1944. Assembled at this meeting were various high-ranking members of the German Army. According to postwar interviews with those present at the September 16 meeting, Hitler's plan was a surprise to most in attendance.

The decision by Hitler to divulge his plans at the last minute reflected his general distrust of his top military advisors. This lack of trust had a lot to do with the abortive July 20, 1944, attempt on his life by a small group of disgruntled army officers. Despite this lack of confidence, Hitler still retained the respect and admiration of the Army's rank and file in late 1944.

Between September 16 and October 10, the staff of the German Army presented an initial Operations Plan for the Ardennes counteroffensive for Hitler's approval. Hitler approved the concept the next day and ordered that detailed planning be undertaken to prepare for what became the last grand endeavor of the German military in World War II.

Fully aware that preparations for such a large offensive operation would be hard to hide from the Western Allies or even his own troops, Hitler and a select group of high-ranking senior officers devised a number of steps to fool everybody into thinking the build-up of forces along the western front was strictly defensive in nature. These decoy activities included the creation of a phantom army, referred to as the Twenty-fifth, composed of 10 divisions. This was achieved by extensive and realistic radio traffic in the area in which the force was supposedly stationed. As an added safety precaution, no

The most important factor that influenced Hitler's decision to attack in the Ardennes was the Allied advance across France to the German border, between August and September 1944. Hitler considered this a more pressing danger to Germany than the Soviet advance in the east. The American crew of a .30-caliber (air-cooled) machine gun, fires at German positions somewhere in France. *National Archives*

On the western front, the Americans had, in the second week of September 1944, crossed the German border and advanced on the German city of Aachen. At the same time, the British and Canadian armies had entered Holland. The German armies in the west therefore faced an Allied front that extended from the Swiss border to the North Sea. American soldiers take a joy ride on a German Tiger II heavy tank captured near Aachen. *National Archives*

radio transmissions regarding the real plans for Hitler's Ardennes counteroffensive were allowed. Documents regarding the plans were hand-delivered by specially picked military couriers, escorted by Gestapo agents. (This decision did much to rob the Allies of information from German military radio codes.)

The process by which the Allies could read the German signal traffic was code-named "Ultra." Prior to late 1944, Ultra intercepts gave valuable advance warning to American and British military commanders of a majority of German military plans. This knowledge allowed Allied generals to dramatically shorten the war by keeping one step ahead of their German opponents.

Despite strong suspicions that the Allies had managed to obtain secret information from unknown sources, the Germans remained convinced throughout the war that their radio signal codes were completely secure. The delivery of Ardennes counteroffensive documents by human couriers was seen by the Germans as an added safeguard before any leaks could be pinpointed and eliminated.

Beginning in August 1944, Hitler started laying the groundwork for the "Watch on the Rhine" operation, by giving the western front

Hitler was not nearly as discouraged about the situation in September 1944 as were his senior generals. He could clearly see that the rapid Allied advance across France was running out of steam as its supply lines became stretched to the breaking point. The Siegfried Line had not yet been seriously breached, and the Soviet summer offensive seemed to have run its course. A squad of German infantry is armed with panzerfausts (single-shot recoilless antitank grenade launchers) that had successfully ambushed and destroyed a Soviet tank. *Author's collection*

priority in tanks and artillery. Hitler's top generals strongly objected to this tactic, believing that the equipment should be sent to the hard-pressed German divisions fighting the Soviet armies on the eastern front.

By September 5, the Soviet Summer Offensive, launched shortly after the Allied invasion of Normandy in June 1944, had reached the borders of East Prussia, only 300 miles from Berlin. To slow the Soviet juggernaut, the Germans had been forced to commit more than two million men to the eastern front. In contrast, only about 700,000 men were deployed against the Western Allies. German losses on the eastern front between June and August 1944 were estimated to be over 900,000.

Fortunately for Hitler, the spectacular Soviet Summer Offensive had outrun its supply lines by the first week of September 1944 and had ground to a halt. Another factor that slowed the Russian advance was the beginning of heavy autumn rains. These rains turned the flat plains of Poland into a soggy mess, unable to support the American-built supply trucks used by the Soviets to keep their armies moving forward.

In the Balkans, the Soviet armies had successfully occupied Bulgaria and Romania, and were rapidly approaching Hungary. This advance threatened to cut off the German forces and forced Hitler to order the evacuation of Greece and Albania. With the capture of Romania, the Soviets took over the important oil refineries at Ploesti, cutting the German war machine off from one of its last major sources of fuel.

Near the end of the Soviet Summer Offensive, Hitler became increasingly aware of the great threat posed by the American and British armies on the western front. The Western Allies had liberated all of northern France and the greater part of Belgium and Luxembourg by the middle of September 1944. U.S. Army units had entered Germany's Trier region on September 11 and the Aachen area on September 12. The Ruhr, the industrial heart of Germany, now lay within striking distance of the Allied armies.

The senior leadership of the German Army had no doubts about the seriousness of the situation facing Germany at this point in the war. Many believed the war was already lost. For Hitler, a man with an incredible mystical belief in his own military genius, just the opposite occurred. He soon decided that desperate times called for desperate measures.

Hitler decided to build up a force strong enough to counter the advance of the American and British armies, and commanded the creation of an operational reserve of 25 new infantry divisions for use as he saw fit on the western front.

To rebuild his armored reserves on the western front, Hitler ordered what was left of the Waffen SS panzer divisions to be pulled out of service in France and turned over to the command of a new army headquarters referred to as the Sixth Panzer Army. Once in reserve, the panzer divisions were to be refitted and brought quickly up to full strength.

## Allied Military Problems

Despite the numerous setbacks suffered by Hitler's armies on the western front between June and September 1944, the British and American armies had their own problems. One of the biggest missteps occurred when the British 11th Armored Division captured intact the vital inland Belgian harbor of Antwerp on September 4, 1944, but failed to secure the 65-mile-long Schelde Estuary that connected Antwerp to the North Sea. (The British 11th Armored Division was part of the 21st Army Group under the command of Field Marshal Bernard Montgomery.)

The blame for this missed opportunity lay squarely on the shoulders of Montgomery and American General of the Army Dwight D. Eisenhower. Eisenhower had assumed direct operational command of all the Allied field

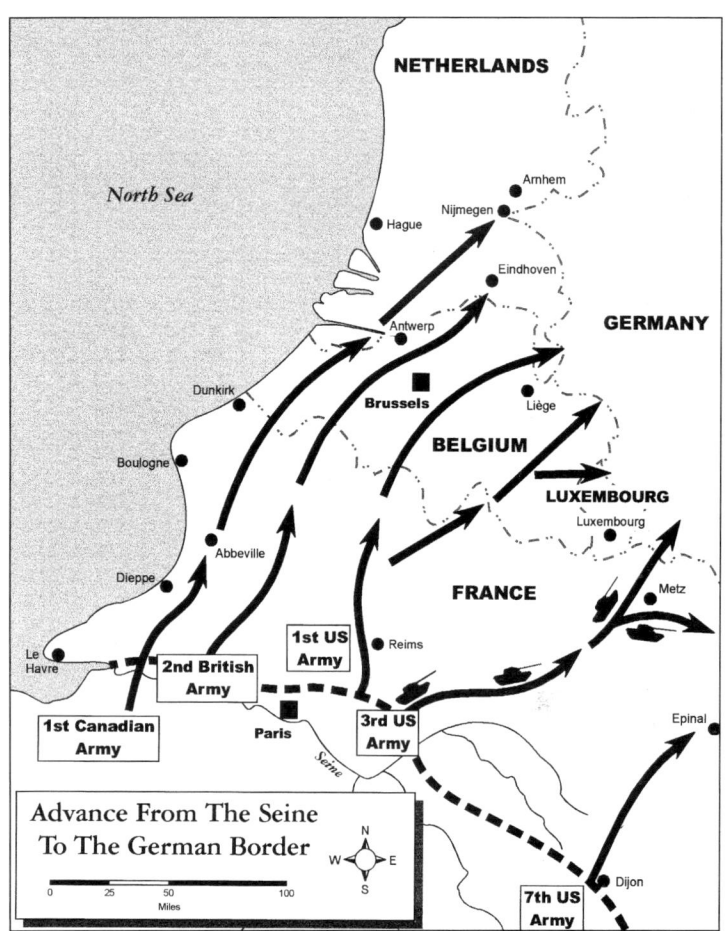

armies from Montgomery on September 1, 1944. Prior to that date, Montgomery was the pro tem commander of all Allied ground forces in northwest Europe. During the fast-paced and unexpected advance of the Allied armies across France during August, the Allies had failed to make the capture of the Schelde Estuary a sufficient priority until it was too late.

Unfortunately, both commanders had let down their guard in light of the widespread belief that the war with Germany was almost over. This belief was somewhat shaken during the last couple of weeks of September, when German resistance along the entire western front stiffened considerably. This quick turn of events caught senior American and British military officers off guard. Throughout the war in western Europe, the Allies were continually surprised by the ability of German ground forces, down to platoon level, to quickly bounce back from almost any situation. Hitler's Ardennes counteroffensive of December 1944 would be the final and best example of that skill.

Even the total Allied superiority in the air had yet to force the Germans to sue for peace, as so many proponents of air power had confidently predicted. Despite massive aerial raids with up to 5,000, planes the German will to resist and the means of resistance remained quite sufficient for a continuation of the war. Bombs of an American aerial raid explode on a German target. *National Archives*

Hitler's awareness of Antwerp's importance hit home when the city fell into British hands on September 4. It took another week or so before the full importance of Antwerp became clear to Eisenhower, as he saw the chance of ending the war by late 1944 disappear. Finally, in a series of high level meetings during the second week of September, Eisenhower confirmed the view that "the early winning of deep water ports and improved maintenance facilities in our rear are prerequisites to a final all-out assault on Germany proper."

Eisenhower had become keenly aware of the fact that his field armies still received the majority of their supplies via the original Normandy invasion beaches. He knew that a spell of bad weather over the English Channel could easily bring the Allied supply system to an abrupt halt.

Another item on Eisenhower's mind was the fact that the Allied armies had advanced much farther than predicted in the original

On September 1, 1944, the Western Allied air strength consisted of 8,785 first-line aircraft. In contrast, the total number of first-line aircraft in the Luftwaffe (including every type) in early September 1944 was estimated to number 6,232 aircraft, of which only 4,507 were serviceable. Me-109 fighter planes are abandoned on a captured German airfield. *National Archives*

10   PATTON AND THE BATTLE OF THE BULGE

In the late summer of 1944, the Allied air forces began to direct their bombs against German armored vehicle factories. They would prove to be an appealing target because of the limited number of final assembly plants. Outside a destroyed German tank factory are a number of Mark III medium tanks. *National Archives*

preinvasion plans. Less than 90 days after the American First Army had landed on the beaches of Normandy, it had advanced to the German border. By September 11, 1944, the Allies had reached a position that preinvasion planners had projected for May 2, 1945, at the earliest.

Unfortunately, the logistical system planned for use in France by the Allies was incapable of handling the accelerated tempo of operations. In preinvasion meetings, the Allied commanders had agreed the Germans would no doubt force their armies to stop at the Seine River. They had planned to use this pause in operations to refit their armies and set up a logistical infrastructure to support the final drive on Germany.

However, in order to take advantage of the disintegration of the German Army in France, Eisenhower did not stop at the Seine. This crucial decision prevented the Allied establishment

For the German war economy, the only area in which the Allied aerial bombing campaign was having a serious near-time affect was in the synthetic oil and ammunition industries. The German armies were soon faced with a looming crisis that would rob them of fuel for their vehicles and ammunition for their guns. German tankers refuel their Mark V Panther medium tank. *Patton Museum*

OPENING MOVES

11

of a logistical system sufficient to meet all the demands that would be placed upon it.

In mid-September 1944, Montgomery's 21st Army Group, which formed the left wing of the Allied front lines, consisted of the First Canadian Army (6 divisions) and the British Second Army (10 divisions). The First Canadian Army was under the command of General Henry D. G. Crerar. The British Second Army was under the command of Lieutenant General Sir Miles C. Dempsy.

The flat lands of Holland and the numerous waterways that crisscrossed most of the country lay between Montgomery's 21st Army Group and Germany. In addition, three easily defensible rivers, the Maas, the Waal, and the Neder Rijn, run through Holland. The portion of the Maas that runs through Belgium is referred to as the Meuse. All three rivers are lower branches of the Rhine River in Germany.

Aware of the looming logistic crisis about to catch up with the Allied armies in mid-September, Montgomery and Eisenhower decided on September 10, to briefly defer their emphasis on the 21st Army Group's seizure of the 65-mile-long Schelde Estuary. Instead, at Eisenhower's insistence, Montgomery decided to use the First Allied Airborne Army, under the command of Lieutenant General Lewis H. Brereton, to capitalize on German disorganization. This would be achieved by launching a large aerial attack, code-named Operation Market Garden, to capture three key Dutch bridges over the rivers Maas, Waal, and Neder Rijn at Grave, Nijmegen, and Arnhem.

Operation Market Garden, ill-conceived and poorly planned, began on September 17 with approximately 20,000 paratroopers and glider troops landing in the largest airborne assault of the entire war. Unfortunately, Montgomery, in

The German railway system had been under sporadic air attacks for years but remained an ongoing concern. Still, the Germans knew it would be only a matter of time before the Allied air forces turned their interests to this important transportation asset. With that thought in mind, Hitler's advisors informed him that the German railroad system could support one final major attack before the close of 1944. In the middle of a destroyed German rail yard are railroad cars carrying the turrets from Mark V Panther medium tanks. *National Archives*

In spite of the heavy losses suffered by the Wehrmacht on both the eastern and western fronts, Hitler was certain that replacements could be found and new divisions created. He appointed Heinrich Himmler, the long-time head of the dreaded SS, chief of the Replacement Army. He also entrusted his long time propaganda chief, Joseph Goebbels, with a comb-out program designed to sweep up all available manpower that had not yet been drafted into front-line military service. Together at a prewar ceremony are Hitler (standing in the vehicle) and Himmler, saluting his leader. *Real War Photos*

Himmler and Goebbels, by scraping the bottom of the German manpower barrel in July and August 1944, managed to create 18 new infantry divisions, 10 panzer brigades, and nearly 100 separate infantry battalions. Hitler then insisted on September 10, 1944, that the two men deliver in October and November 1944 at least 25 new infantry divisions for use in his Ardennes counteroffensive. These German soldiers await the signal to advance. *National Archives*

his haste to launch the operation, ignored crucial intelligence that identified two refitted Waffen SS panzer divisions, bivouacked in the target area. The German armored units cut the Allied airborne units to pieces, and the British army's First Airborne Division was almost completely destroyed. The ground assault phase of Operation Market Garden, undertaken by the British Second Army, also ran into unexpected stiff German resistance and made little progress.

One of the unforeseen problems that arose after the failure of Operation Market Garden was the creation of a wide gap between the British Second Army and the American First Army on its right flank. The First Army, in the center of the Allied front lines, was forced to stretch its already thin resources to cover the gap. The significance of this lengthening of the First Army's front lines would become very apparent to Eisenhower when Hitler launched his Ardennes counteroffensive a little over two months later.

## Opposing Forces

The First Army was part of the American 12th Army Group in eastern France, under the command of Lieutenant General Omar N. Bradley, and consisted of the First and Third Armies. The First Army, under the command of Lieutenant General Courtney H. Hodges, consisted of eight divisions, three armor and five infantry. The eight divisions of the First Army and various attached nondivisional units were divided into three corps, the V, VII, and XIX) and were deployed along a 65-mile front.

The XIX and the VII Corps of the First Army were assigned the task of advancing in a northeastern direction to fill the gap in the Allied front line left by Montgomery's 21st Army Group. The V Corps had orders to advance eastward in the same general direction as the Third Army. The Third Army was on the right flank of the First Army, south of the Ardennes, slowly advancing eastward on a front about 90 miles wide toward the Saar region of Germany. Behind the Saar lay the Rhine, an important Third Army objective.

The Third Army was under the command of Lieutenant General George S. Patton. The always-colorful and flamboyant Patton pushed the Third Army to move more forcefully than any other army during August, when the German military forces in France began to crumble.

On September 1, 1944, General Dwight D. Eisenhower, the supreme Allied commander, had a total of 38 divisions in northwest Europe. A smiling Eisenhower gets ready to visit some of his front line units in a jeep. *National Archives*

The commander of the 21st Army Group was Field Marshal Sir Bernard Law Montgomery. His best-known claim to fame occurred as commander of the British Eighth Army in North Africa in 1942–1943. Well liked by the common British soldier and the British public, Montgomery, here in the commander's position in a tank somewhere in North Africa, was roundly detested by his American military leadership for his overly cautious form of command. *National Archives*

OPENING MOVES

Between Montgomery's 21st Army Group and its final destination, Germany, lay the flat lands of Holland and the numerous waterways that crisscrossed most of the country. In addition, three easily defensible rivers, the Maas, the Waal, and the Neder Rijn ran through Holland. All three rivers were lower branches of the Rhine River in Germany. This British-built ACE Armored Car Mark III is armed with a 75-millimeter gun and has a crew of four men. *British Army Tank Museum*

Montgomery and Eisenhower decided on September 10, 1944, to briefly defer their emphasis on the seizure of the 65-mile-long Schelde Estuary that connects the port of Antwerp to the sea. Instead, they decided to launch a large aerial attack, code-named Operation Market Garden, to capture three key Dutch bridges over the rivers Maas, Waal, and Neder Rijn at Grave, Nijmegen, and Arnhem. Within the confines of a C-47 cargo plane, a group of American paratroopers is ready to depart on a mission. *National Archives*

Unfortunately, the success of Patton and the rapidly advancing divisions of his Third Army imposed a severe strain on the unprepared Allied logistical system.

On September 12, Eisenhower assumed direct command of the 6th Army Group, under General Jacob L. Devers, as it was coming up from southern France. The 6th Army Group would take its place to the right of Patton's Third Army. With the addition of the 6th Army Group, Eisenhower gained three American infantry divisions, an airborne task force of approximately divisional size, and seven American-equipped Free French divisions (two armor and five infantry).

Despite the addition of Devers' divisions in mid-September 1944, Eisenhower lacked sufficient reserve divisions in Europe. This problem had a lot to do with Eisenhower's commitment to a "broad front" strategy toward Germany. Eisenhower believed that

## MILITARY ORGANIZATIONS

Within the World War II U.S. Army command structure, field armies served as tactical and administrative organizations which directed from one to four corps. Corps, in turn, directed from one to five divisions. A very similar organizational structure also existed within the British, Canadian, and German armies of World War II.

The only permanent part of a field army was the headquarters staff and some communication (signal) and administrative (clerical) units. To oversee field armies on both sides, there was a higher level of command known as the army group. The American army had two army groups operating by September 1944. The British and Canadians formed a single army group in western Europe. The Germans countered by organizing their field armies into three army groups for fighting the Allies in western Europe.

Corps tend to be very flexible organizations designed to direct any combination of divisions. During World War II, the U.S. Army would form 24 corps, of which 23 saw action overseas. A typical U.S. Army corps in northwest Europe in 1944–45 consisted of one armored division and two infantry divisions.

Aerial attacks by the Allied airborne forces beginning on September 17, 1944 on the three key Dutch bridges were supported on the ground by a British armored division. The job of the armored division was to link up with the lightly armed paratroopers as quickly as possible, before the Germans could bring in reinforcements. Like their airborne counterparts, the British tankers met stiff and unexpected German resistance that delayed their advance. Pictured in Europe is a British-built Cromwell medium tank, armed with a 75-millimeter gun. *British Army Tank Museum*

Since the Allied logistical system could not bring up enough supplies to support large-scale offensive operations by both the British and American field armies at the same time, Eisenhower reduced the amount of supplies, especially gasoline, to Patton's Third Army. Eisenhower and Patton, together here for an awards ceremony, had shared a warm friendship that by late 1944 had been badly strained by the pressures of wartime command. *National Archives*

this would force the Germans to stretch their ground forces thin along the front lines, and would keep them guessing about the next Allied offensive.

If Montgomery's 21st Army Group launched an attack in the northern sector of the western front, the Germans would not be able to concentrate their reserve forces to repel that attack, out of fear that Bradley's 12th Army Group or Devers' Sixth Army Group would launch an attack in the southern sector.

Eisenhower hoped that this strategy would also prevent the German ground forces from being able to concentrate enough divisions to launch a counteroffensive. The biggest fault with this plan was that the Allied armies, with

On August 30, 1944, the 12th Army Group officially notified the Third Army that it would be supplied with no more gasoline until September 3. On the day before, many of Patton's leading armored units were already out of fuel. An American M-10 tank destroyer is in a hull-down defensive position somewhere in France in 1944. *National Archives*

Above and below: The fuel crisis that hit the Third Army in late August and early September was not to be the first time that Patton had supply troubles. When his Third Army was involved in overrunning the interior of the Brittany peninsula of France in early August, Patton had numerous problems acquiring the proper amount of fuel, ammunition, and other supplies needed to keep its highly mobile forces on the move. American M-12 self-propelled 155-millimeter howitzers fire at German positions. *National Archives*

only 49 divisions, could not adequately man the entire western front.

The Allies thought that the Germans had deployed 48 infantry divisions, 15 panzer-type divisions and several independent panzer brigades to oppose Eisenhower's forces. In reality, the Germans had far fewer divisions on the western front and were badly undermanned. A high-ranking German general estimated that the German forces facing Eisenhower in mid-September 1944 were equivalent to half the number of Allied divisions. The Germans did have the advantage of shorter supply lines, because they had been on the defensive during a period of very poor weather. They also had combat-experienced troops, some better weapons, and they were better positioned behind

OPENING MOVES 19

When Patton's Third Army turned its attention eastward and sped off in the direction of the Seine River, a new crisis arose. There were not enough trucks to resupply the Third Army as it moved deeper into central France at a speed of 40 miles a day. At one point during the dash across France, Patton was forced to hold back one of his corps to conserve enough fuel to keep his other corps moving. U.S. Army engineers are erecting a temporary bridge across the Seine River. *National Archives*

natural and man-made obstacles that slowed down the Allied advance.

In September 1944 the British Army was facing its own manpower problems. Having a far smaller population to draw from than the American army, it struggled to maintain the 10 divisions it already had in northwestern Europe. This problem was compounded by the heavy losses the British army took in the early part of the war.

The shortage of British and American divisions forced Eisenhower and Bradley to thin out the American forces in positions where German offensive operations were highly

Keeping supplies, mostly gasoline, flowing to Patton's Third Army at the end of August 1944 was not easy. Eisenhower approved the creation of a temporary airlift, using almost 1,000 troop carrier planes and large four-engine bombers to fly supplies to the forward elements of the Third Army. *Real War Photos*

The Allied preinvasion planners had optimistically hoped to utilize the French railroad system to move supplies to its advancing armies. Heavy damage inflicted on the railroad system west of the Seine River, by Allied air power and French Resistance forces, made this plan unrealistic until extensive and time-consuming rebuilding could be completed. Taken from an American heavy bomber, this dramatic photo shows a French railroad yard under heavy attack. *Real War Photos*

Another stop-gap measure put into place at the same time involved stripping trucks from other U.S. Army units in France, and assigning them to a special supply unit nicknamed the "Red Ball Express." By running these supply trucks 24 hours a day along certain specially designated one-way routes through France, the Third Army was able to receive at least a basic minimum of its required supplies. An American MP, on his Harley-Davidson motorcycle, is giving directions to the driver of an Army truck. *National Archives*

## U.S. Army Personnel Shortfalls

The shortage of U.S. Army divisions in Europe did not develop overnight. Even before the Japanese attack on Pearl Harbor, America's senior military leaders were already trying to figure out the number of divisions the army would need to fight and win a global conflict, in which they expected to be involved. Since it took at least a year to properly train a single infantry division, the Army had to coordinate with American industry well in advance to begin production of the

unlikely. Unfortunately for Eisenhower, it did not take long for the Germans to notice the thinness of the American lines in the Ardennes, and they rearranged their own front lines in response.

Eisenhower called Bradley, Patton, Hodges, and Major General Hoyt Vanderberg, the new commander of the Ninth Air Force, to his headquarters on September 2, 1944, for a meeting. During this meeting, Eisenhower informed his assembled guests that as soon as the two First Army corps completed the move north in support of Montgomery's 21st Army Group, both the First and Third Armies would discontinue their eastward advance. Pictured is an American M-8 Armored Car somewhere in Europe. *National Archives*

22  PATTON AND THE BATTLE OF THE BULGE

In order to reassure his field commanders that the halt of the American First and Third Armies was only a temporary change in plans, Eisenhower told them that as soon as sufficient gasoline and other supplies became available, the Third Army and the V Corps of the First Army would be ordered to continue their eastward advance and seize those segments of the Siegfried Line within their respective sectors of operations. This M-18 tank destroyer, nicknamed the Hellcat, is armed with a high-velocity 76-millimeter gun. *National Archives*

necessary weapons and equipment to outfit its proposed divisions.

In the fall of 1941, the U.S. War Department had projected an army with a peak strength of 213 divisions. This figure was based on the premise that the Germans would knock the Soviet Union out of the war in 1941 or 1942. As time went on, it became clear that the Soviet Union was in for the long haul. The War Department revised its projected need for divisions down to 120–125 in early 1943, on the correct assumption that the bulk of the German ground forces would be deployed on the eastern front, fighting the massive Soviet army of over 400 divisions. By late 1943 German defeats on the eastern front convinced the War Department to once again reduce its projections on the number of divisions needed to beat Germany and Japan down to 90.

Plans for an additional 15 infantry divisions to be set up in 1944 were shelved, due to a serious shortage of service troops during 1944 for the war against Japan, and also a shortage of men to operate the Army Air Force's growing number of B-29 bombers. Another problem that hampered the army's efforts to find enough men to fill out its divisions was its need to compete for manpower with the other services, such as the navy and the marines.

Overshadowing all these problems in providing the army with sufficient divisions to fulfill its missions, and in building up a strategic

OPENING MOVES 23

On September 11, 1944, a patrol from the Third Army made contact with French army units belonging to the American 6th Army Group, advancing up from the south of France. The 6th Army Group, under the command of Lieutenant General Jacob L. Devers, consisted of the American Seventh Army and the French First Army. An American soldier takes the time to clean his M-1 Garand rifle before the next battle. *National Archives*

reserve to cope with emergencies, was America's role as the great "Arsenal of Democracy." This role dictated that the armed services could not have more than 7.8 percent of the available 15 to 16 million men fit for military service during World War II. Exceeding this ceiling would restrict the development of America's war production capacity. This meant that American military manpower calculations were closely correlated with the needs of its war industry throughout World War II.

On September 21, 1944, the official hookup between Patton's Third Army and Devers' 6th Army Group took place. The Allies' front line facing Germany now ran unbroken from the northern border of neutral Switzerland to the North Sea, a distance of 625 miles. Pictured is an American 81-millimeter mortar and crew. It could fire a roughly 7-pound round out to a range of almost 3,290 yards. *National Archives*

The three divisions of Patton's VIII Corps, under the command of Major General Troy Middleton, did not take part in the advance across France. They were left behind with the task of capturing the German-held port of Brest, located on the tip of the Brittany peninsula. An American soldier inspects an abandoned German 20-millimeter antiaircraft gun mounted on a two-wheel towed trailer. *National Archives*

Not everybody was happy with the risks entailed in deploying an army of only 90 divisions. A month before the Allies launched their invasion of the continent, Secretary of War Henry L. Stimson wrote to General George C. Marshall, chief of staff of the army and chairman of the Joint Chiefs of Staff. In his letter he said, "I have always felt that our contribution to the war should include so far as possible an overwhelming appearance of national strength when we actually get into the critical battle. By this I mean not merely strength on the battle front but in reserve...."

On the last day of August 1944, Patton's XX and XII Corps managed to seize bridgeheads across the Meuse River, in the French province of Lorraine. These American soldiers are carrying a lightweight wooden assault boat to one of the river crossing sites. *National Archives*

OPENING MOVES 25

## BATTLEFIELD GEOGRAPHY LESSON

The most important objective for the western Allied commanders in late 1944 was the Rhine River. It was felt that once the Allied armies got across the river into the heart of Germany, Hitler's dream of world conquest would be vanquished for all time.

The Rhine springs from three glacier-fed streams in the Swiss Alps, flows through Lake Constance in Switzerland, and then travels on a northwesterly course into Germany. The river is, on average, a quarter-mile wide at an average depth of 28 feet. Eight hundred miles from its headwaters, the Rhine empties into the North Sea through three estuaries in Holland.

In its 300-mile course through Germany, the Rhine passes through five different provinces collectively referred to as the Rhineland. The Moselle and the Main Rivers also flow through the Rhineland. Within the Rhineland are the important German industrial areas of the Ruhr and the Saar.

In late 1944, the Ruhr and the Saar were prime objectives of Eisenhower's Allied armies. Of the two industrial areas, the Ruhr was the larger and more important in terms of industrial might. Mongtomery's 21st Army Group and a large part of Hodges' First Army were aiming for the Ruhr, while the objective of Patton's Third Army was the Saar.

The Ruhr, which is neither a political nor geographical entity, is located north of the Ardennes in northwestern Germany. The area surrounding the Ruhr is roughly 2,000 square miles and includes the major German factory cities of Essen, Düsseldorf, and Wuppertal. Without the Ruhr, Germany's ability to produce the weapons of war needed by its armies would be severely crippled.

The industrial center of the Saar, and the area surrounding it, encompasses almost 3,000 square miles. The Saar is located south of the Ardennes and west of Germany's Rhine. Mines located in the Saar provided a great deal of the coal needed by the German factories in the Ruhr. By late 1944, one of the few synthetic oil plants still functioning in Germany was located in the Saar. In addition, the Saar was the home of Germany's I.G. Farben plant, which produced 40 to 50 percent of the country's chemical output. Chemicals are the basic building blocks of all explosives and a crucial part of the war-making ability of any country.

Other than Arlon and the capital City of Luxembourg, there are no major cities in the Ardennes. In late 1944, the area was dotted by a number of small villages with populations between 2,500 to 4,000. Many of the villages consisted of only a single farm or inn that gave its name to the crossroads at which it stood.

The Ardennes is officially divided into two parts. The smaller Low Ardennes is in the northwest, and the High Ardennes lies in the northeast, center, and south. The High Ardennes makes up some three-fourths of the entire region and includes the northeastern Belgian towns of Spa and Malmèdy. Also found in this area is the Belgian town of St. Vith, located very close to the German border.

The Belgian town of Bastogne lies in the center section of the High Ardennes. Both St. Vith and Bastogne would play important roles in the Battle of the Bulge, since all of the major roads in the High Ardennes passed through these small villages. A number of excellent hard surface roads crossed the Ardennes area from north to south. In contrast, there was not a single major highway crossing the Ardennes in a direct east-west direction.

German and American military commanders knew that cross-country movement by military vehicles in the High Ardennes was extremely limited in even the best weather. In times of rain, the soil in the Ardennes turns into thick mud, and heavy armored vehicles could not move cross-country unless the ground was frozen. This made the possession of the road centers of St. Vith and Bastogne crucial to the control of the High Ardennes.

On their way to Antwerp through the High Ardennes, the Germans had to cross the Meuse River and several other major rivers, including the Amblève, the Salm, and the Ourthe. The Ourthe River originates west of Bastogne as a small creek and flows northward until it meets the Meuse River at the Belgium city of Liege. The Ourthe was a very difficult military obstacle for a large German mechanized force. The rugged nature of the High

Ardennes region through which the Ourthe flows causes crossing sites to be few and extremely narrow. This leads to channeling large troop movements in either direction, limiting the freedom of maneuver for a mechanized force and giving local defenders a big advantage. Beyond the Ourthe, the only other rivers before the Meuse were the Lesse and L' Hommel, neither of which posed serious crossing problems for the German mechanized forces. However, the Meuse was a serious military obstacle for the Germans, as it offered excellent defensive opportunities for enemy forces. The Meuse flows northerly through Belgium and France, roughly 100 yards wide, with steep cliffs up to 700 feet high along the greater part of its course. The section of the Meuse that the Germans needed to cross lay between the cities of Liège and Namur in Belgium, only 60 miles away from the ultimate German objective, Antwerp.

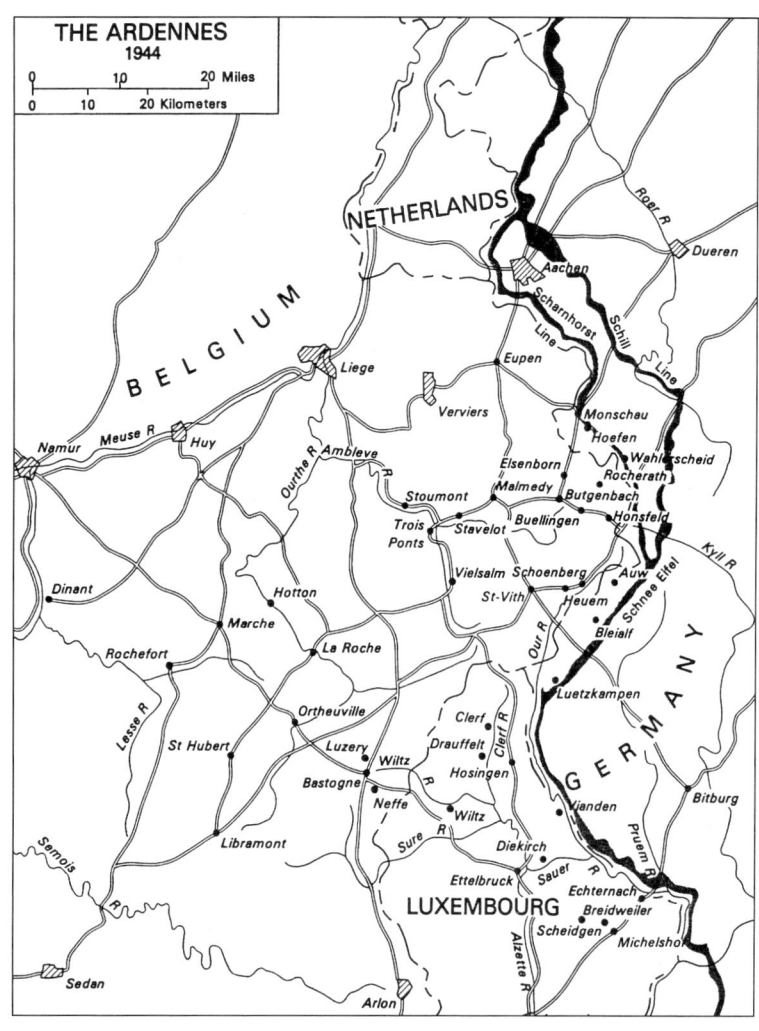

The continuation of the Ardennes forests within Germany is referred to as the Eifel Ranges. The Eifel Ranges form a part of the German Rhineland consisting of a complex of hills lying between the Rhine, the Moselle, and the Roer Rivers. The Germans used the two westernmost of the many hill ranges that make up the area to hide their military preparations for the Ardennes counteroffensive. The Germans were concentrated in an area known as the Schnee Eifel, east of St. Vith and just inside the German border, and another area north of it referred to as the Hohes Venn. Due to German pre–World War I construction in the Schnee Eifel, the region had an extensive rail and road network, which greatly aided the secret German military buildup in late 1944.

The rugged geography of the Eifel-Ardennes region limited the Germans to launching a large westward advance across the Meuse River to Antwerp at only three locations. One was in the Low Ardennes. The second was farther south in the High Ardennes between Monschau and the Losheim Gap. A westward advance from this location would require the Germans to capture the Belgian towns of Malmèdy and St. Vith before attempting to advance on their final objectives. The third location was even farther south, in the area between the German cities of Prum and Trier. This location offered the Germans the largest base of operations for their forces, but was the farthest away from the Meuse and Antwerp.

OPENING MOVES 27

Having served as an artillery officer with the U.S. Army in France during World War I, Stimson knew firsthand how the modern weapons of war could inflict heavy casualties on frontline soldiers. Army calculations on the number of men that would be needed to replace losses from combat seemed in his opinion "to shave the line of sufficiency rather narrowly, instead of aiming at massive abundance." Stimson feared that the army would not deploy enough divisions to Europe, or keep enough in reserve, to ensure victory. Against the estimated 56 German divisions that were to defend France, the U.S. Army would have barely more than an equal number available for offensive operation in Europe by the end of that summer.

It is a widely accepted and long-standing military maxim that an attacking force should always have at least a three-to-one, or greater, advantage over a defending force to ensure

Worried by Patton's bridgeheads across the Meuse River, Hitler instructed the German commander of the western front that he wanted a large armored counterattack launched at the southern flank of Patton's forces in Lorraine. Hitler was convinced that Patton's Third Army was leading the main advance on Germany and would soon pass through the Siegfried Line into the industrial area of the Saar. Somewhere on the line, an American soldier checks the military ID papers of a dead German soldier. *National Archives*

Following Hitler's orders, the German Army mounted a somewhat hasty series of counterattacks against Patton's Third Army between September 19 and October 11, 1944. Patton's now battle-hardened troops threw the counterattacks back, inflicting heavy losses in both men and equipment. These two Mark V Panther medium tanks were a small part of the equipment the Germans lost in combat during the fighting in the Lorraine. *Patton Museum*

This Canadian-built Ram tank, basically a copy of the American-built M-3 medium tank, was converted into an armored personnel carrier by removal of its gun-armed turret. In its modified configuration the vehicle was named the Kangaroo and could carry 11 infantrymen. It was employed by both the Canadian and British armies in Europe. *British Army Tank Museum*

success. Based on this premise, Stimson accurately predicted that a stalemate might develop in Europe when fall and winter conditions reduced the army's ability to maneuver. Marshall tried to reassure Stimson before D-Day that Allied air superiority in Europe and the high quality of American ground combat units would make up for any disadvantage in numbers.

In the end, both men were partially correct. Allied airpower would prove to be a very effective force-multiplier in the European theater of operations, weather permitting.

Another problem for the U.S. Army senior planners that cropped up soon after the Normandy landings was the unexpected high losses among the infantry. This shortage of infantry would result in the army taking drastic measures to acquire the men it needed. This

At the end of October 1944, both sides licked their wounds and prepared for future operations. The Germans took this opportunity to continue improving their defensive positions that faced Patton's Third Army in eastern France. Pictured are the destroyed remains of a German self-propelled 105-millimeter howitzer, designated the Hummel (bumble-bee). *National Archives*

OPENING MOVES 29

Besides Antwerp, Montgomery was also ordered to capture other northwest Channel ports before winter storms rendered the beaches in Normandy unusable. As part of his armored forces, Montgomery had the American-built M-4 Sherman tank modified by the British to mount a high-velocity 76.2-millimeter antitank gun. In British and Canadian service, it was known as the Sherman VC Firefly, pictured here at left and below. *British Army Tank Museum*

included the repeated culling of any rear-area troops that could be spared.

Stimson proved to be uncomfortably close on his call about the army cutting the number of divisions too close for comfort. The launching of Hitler's Ardennes operation almost pushed the American army in western Europe to the breaking point. It fell to the divisions of

Despite Eisenhower's strong urgings and additional supplies, the First Canadian Army, part of Montgomery's 21st Army Group, made little headway in its efforts to clear the approaches to Antwerp. The Canadians had begun to drive north from Antwerp on October 2, 1944. On their right, troops of the I British Corps also advanced northward to cover the right flank of the First Canadian Army. Pictured is a column of American-built M-5 light tanks in British service. *British Army Tank Museum*

The most difficult Canadian objective within the Schelde Estuary was the German-held Island of Walcheren, some 50 miles east of Antwerp. It was the last barrier between Allied supply ships and Antwerp. These two American soldiers are posing with one of the largest weapons employed by the Germans in its defense, the Flak 40 128-millimeter gun, used as an antiaircraft gun. *National Archives*

By early October 1944, Eisenhower began losing his patience with Montgomery's lack of success in opening up Antwerp to shipping traffic. Montgomery, here reviewing a map with another British senior officer, took the hint and began to devote most of his remaining resources to clearing the Schelde Estuary. *Patton Museum*

Montgomery's 21st Army Group to provide a backstop to the hard-pressed divisions of Bradley's 12th Army Group at the height of the Battle of the Bulge.

As the fighting continued in the Ardennes, the army rushed every remaining division in the United States to Europe, leaving it without any strategic reserve in case of another crisis. Fortunately for the American army and Eisenhower, Hitler had shot his last bolt with the Ardennes counteroffensive and had nothing left with which to mount another offensive operation.

## Patton's Third Army Problems

A hard-to-solve problem for Eisenhower was the inability of the Allied logistical system to bring up enough supplies to support large-scale offensive operations by both Montgomery's and Bradley's field armies at the same time. Eisenhower was therefore forced to cut back on the amount of supplies, especially gasoline, to the Third Army.

Patton first became aware of this looming fuel shortfall when his staff notified him early on August 29 that the Third Army was not receiving its normal gas supply. Patton quickly went to see Bradley at the 12th Army Group headquarters to ask him for more fuel. Bradley had to refuse Patton's request. The next day, the

12th Army Group officially notified the Third Army that it would be supplied with no more gasoline until September 3. On the day before, many of Patton's leading armored units had already run out of fuel. Patton ordered his men to drain the gasoline out of one tank to refuel other tanks, and when all else failed, the tank crews were to get out of their vehicles and walk!

This would not be the first time that Patton had had supply troubles. When his Third Army was involved in overrunning the interior of the Brittany peninsula of France in early August 1944, Patton had numerous problems in acquiring the fuel, ammunition, and other supplies needed to keep his highly mobile forces on the move.

As the Third Army turned its attention eastward and sped off in the direction of the Seine River, a new crisis arose. There were not enough trucks to resupply the Third Army as it moved deeper into central France at a speed of 40 miles per day. At one point during the dash across France, Patton was forced to hold back one of his corps to conserve enough fuel to keep his other corps moving.

The Allied preinvasion planners had optimistically hoped to utilize the French railroad

The Germans never had any doubts about the importance of the port of Antwerp to the Allied cause. The Germans were well aware of Eisenhower's logistical problems, and had accurately predicated in early September that his armies would soon be halted without access to a deep-water port. Typical of the late-war German antitank weapons encountered by Allied tankers was this 88-millimeter gun, fitted on a cruciform mount. *Patton Museum*

Eisenhower's efforts to penetrate the Siegfried Line and reach the Rhine between mid-September and early December 1944 is referred to by U.S. Army historians as the Rhineland Campaign. Along the Siegfried Line, an American bulldozer is being used to bury a large German pillbox to prevent any future use by its former owners. *National Archives*

OPENING MOVES  33

The most unnecessary and least productive of the Rhineland campaigns was fought in the Huertgen Forest of Belgium by the VII Corps of Hodges' First Army. In less than two months, four of the corps' divisions were nearly destroyed and 33,000 of the 120,000 troops involved became casualties. American soldiers in the Huertgen Forest are advancing past the body of a dead German soldier. *Real War Photos*

system to move supplies to its advancing armies. Heavy damage inflicted on the railroad system west of the Seine River, by Allied airpower and French resistance forces, made this plan unrealistic until extensive and time-consuming rebuilding could be completed.

Daily consumption of gasoline for Patton's Third Army during August was about 400,000 gallons. A single American armored division could use up to 100,000 gallons of gasoline in one day of cross-country fighting. To keep supplies (mostly gasoline) flowing to Patton's Third Army at the end of August 1944, Eisenhower approved the creation of a temporary airlift, using almost 1,000 troop carrier planes and large four-engine bombers to fly supplies to the forward elements of the Third Army.

Another stop-gap measure put into place at the same time involved stripping trucks from other U.S. Army units in France, and assigning them to a special supply unit nicknamed the "Red Ball Express." By running these supply

34 PATTON AND THE BATTLE OF THE BULGE

trucks 24 hours a day along certain specially designated one-way routes through France, the Third Army was able to receive at least a basic minimum of its required supplies.

Eisenhower called Bradley, Patton, Hodges, and Major General Hoyt Vanderberg, the new commander of the Ninth Air Force, to his headquarters on September 2, 1944, for a meeting. During this meeting, Eisenhower informed his guests that as soon as the two First Army corps completed the move north in support of Montgomery's 21st Army Group, both the First and Third Armies would discontinue their eastward advance. In order to reassure his field

At the conclusion of the Huertgen Forest Campaign, two of the badly shot-up divisions involved in the fighting, the 4th and 28th Infantry Divisions, were moved to the Ardennes sector of the front in early December to rest and be refitted. Pictured are two American soldiers examining a captured German 50-millimeter light mortar. *National Archives*

The First Army was the not the only one to suffer heavy losses, with little gain, during the Rhineland Campaign. Patton's Third Army would spend 16 brutal weeks fighting in the French province of Lorraine. This American M-7 self-propelled howitzer, commonly nicknamed the Priest, is firing on German positions. The Priest consisted of a 105-millimeter howitzer mounted on a modified chassis of either an M-3 or M-4 medium tank. *National Archives*

OPENING MOVES 35

The effort to reach the Siegfried Line cost Patton's Third Army 55,182 killed, wounded, and missing in action. Factors that contributed to the slow progress of Patton and his Third Army in the Lorraine included an early lack of supplies, stiff German resistance, and the worst rains in that part of France in over half a century. An American soldier, armed with an M-1 Thompson submachine gun, carefully reads a warning sign. *National Archives*

commanders that this was only a temporary change in plans, Eisenhower told them that as soon as sufficient gasoline and other supplies became available, the Third Army and the V Corps of the First Army would be ordered to continue their eastward advance and seize those segments of the Siegfried Line within their sectors of operations. The Allies frontline facing Germany now ran unbroken from the northern border of neutral Switzerland to the North Sea.

Patton's Third Army had roughly 300,000 men and 669 medium tanks at the end of August. The majority of combat elements found within the Third Army were located within 12 divisions (8 infantry and 4 armor). The divisions were divided among four corps headquarters; the XV, XX, XII, and VIII Corps. The XV Corps was transferred to the First Army on August 24, but returned on the August 26.

The three divisions of Patton's VIII Corps, under the command of Major General Troy Middleton, did not take part in the advance across France. They were left behind with the task of capturing the German-held port of Brest, on the tip of the Brittany peninsula. On September 5, Patton's VIII Corps was transferred to the newly formed American Ninth Army, under the command of Lieutenant General William H. Simpson. The Ninth Army would enter the line between the American First Army and the British Second Army in late October. In November, the VIII Corps would pass to the control of Hodges' First Army.

## The Arguments Regarding the Final Advance on Germany

Eisenhower's approval and support of Operation Market Garden reflected preinvasion plans agreed to by the top Allied military leaders of SHAEF. The plan focused the bulk of Allied resources on the northeastern advance of Montgomery's 21st Army Group into Germany. This policy effectively put in abeyance any of the grand plans proposed by Bradley and Patton to drive on to the German border south of the 21st Army Group location.

A very angry and frustrated Patton could not understand why Eisenhower would not deviate from the plan when opportunities arose that Patton thought he could use to shorten the war.

Bradley, Patton's boss, shared the perception that Eisenhower was favoring the British over the U.S. Army in Europe. Bradley would express his displeasure with the existing situation by silently conspiring with Patton to undermine the supreme commander's orders. He did this by encouraging Patton to keep the Third Army moving toward the Siegfried Line, regardless of Eisenhower's orders. Patton needed very little prompting from Bradley to ignore orders from headquarters. Patton was once quoted as saying, "Personally, I fight every order that I do not like, which makes me very unpopular, but successful." It is a shame that nobody dared asked Patton at the time if he would allow his subordinates the same leeway in obeying orders as he allowed himself.

At the same time, Eisenhower was dealing with complaints from his fellow American generals regarding the future direction of the war in western Europe. He was being forced to spend a great deal of his time listening to Montgomery's pleas to be named the official ground force commander. Unfortunately, the temperamental Montgomery had not yet realized that he had already lost the confidence of Eisenhower and other senior American field commanders by this point in the war.

As the Third Army's advance took it across the Seine River and eventually into the French province of Lorraine, it entered an area of France where the railroad system had suffered far less damage than it had on the westward side of the Seine. During the October 1944 lull in the Third Army operations, it would receive 97,955 tons of supplies by rail, including all the gasoline it needed. These American-built railroad cars, designed for use on the French railroad system, are being unloaded from a U.S. Coast Guard vessel. *Coast Guard*

Montgomery was also constantly badgering Eisenhower to throw all Allied logistical support behind the 21st Army Group and launch a single concentrated thrust into Germany along the northeastern route. This tactic would, of course, bring Patton and his Third Army to a complete halt and forfeit any hope for a subsidiary thrust to the German Siegfried Line.

The Siegfried Line (known to the Germans as the Westwall) consisted of an extensive series of somewhat outdated fortifications along the German border. With more than 3,000 mutually supporting pillboxes of varying sizes, it stretched from the Swiss northern border to the southern border of German-occupied Holland. Behind the Siegfried Line lay the Rhine, the last major defensible natural barrier between the Allied armies and the heart of Germany.

In many places, the Siegfried Line took advantage of rivers, lakes, railroad cuts and fills, sharp defiles and other natural obstacles

OPENING MOVES 37

By early November 1944, Patton's Third Army could finally replenish itself in preparation for another large-scale offensive operation. The crew of a German 120-millimeter heavy mortar manhandles its weapon into its firing position. *National Archives*

to slow down an advancing enemy force. In areas of the Line that lacked sufficient natural obstacles, the Germans built rows of pyramid-shaped reinforced concrete antitank projections, nicknamed "dragon's teeth." The number of pillboxes and the depth of the German defenses along the Siegfried Line varied from area to area, with the strongest portion in front of Patton's Third Army.

The second-strongest portion of the Siegfried Line lay in front of the advancing American First Army. It was this portion of the line that protected the German City of Aachen. North of Aachen lay the Aachen Gap, a historic east-west trading route that provided easy passage to the Rhine. By September 20, Aachen was under attack by the First Army on three sides. The Germans resisted bitterly, now that the Allies were advancing onto their country. Hitler ordered that the city be held to the last man. American soldiers first entered Aachen from the east on October 13. After six days of fierce house-to-house fighting, the American infantry had cleared half of the city. The city was now a battered ruin from shelling and aerial bombing. From that point on, German resistance gradually weakened until the defenders surrendered the city on October 21, 1944.

Knowing that he did not have enough divisions to carry out his grand plan to penetrate the German border, Montgomery asked Eisenhower to reassign a large part of Bradley's 12th Army Group to his command. Eisenhower declined Montgomery's request on the basis that the number of German divisions facing Montgomery did not warrant the full force of American field armies. Instead, he ordered Hodges to send two of his three First Army Corps in a northern direction in support of the 21st Army Group around Antwerp. This was a change from the preinvasion plans that had called for the entire First Army to advance eastward toward the Siegfried Line, on the left flank of Patton's Third Army. Like the First Army, the Third Army had as its intermediate goal the Siegfried Line with the Rhine as the final objective.

While Eisenhower may have liked Montgomery's plan for a northeastern advance on Germany, he had a number of reasons for not giving up completely on Patton's subsidiary advance to the east. Most importantly, the sharp blow delivered by the Germans to Montgomery's Operation Market Garden convinced Eisenhower that the enemy ground forces retained enough of a bite to make a single thrust into Germany an uncertain proposition. Eisenhower believed it was better to continue his broad front strategy in order to keep the Germans guessing about the location of the main Allied advance.

To keep Allied field armies supplied required an all-out effort by Allied supply services, so Eisenhower implemented strategies to help them. In mid-September Eisenhower instructed Montgomery to quickly secure the approaches to the port of Antwerp. Montgomery was instructed to capture other northwest European channel ports before winter storms rendered the beaches in Normandy unusable. To accomplish this near-term goal, Montgomery convinced Eisenhower to divert the majority of supplies entering the continent to his 21st Army Group.

Despite Eisenhower's direct involvement and the availability of ample supplies, the First Canadian Army (part of Montgomery's 21st Army Group) made little headway in its efforts to open Antwerp to shipping traffic. By October

Patton was preparing to launch a new offensive operation from Lorraine, aimed at breaking through the Siegfried Line on December 19, 1944. Hitler beat Patton to the punch by launching his Ardennes counteroffensive on December 16 against the VIII Corps of Hodges' First Army. The American crews of a unit of M-10 tank destroyer unit are attending the all-important mail call. *National Archives*

9, 1944, Eisenhower had lost his patience with Montgomery's lack of success and sent a warning message to Montgomery. In this message he stated: "of all our operations on our entire front from Switzerland to the channel, I consider Antwerp of first importance, and I believe that the operations designed to clear up the entrance require your personal attention." Montgomery took the hint and began to devote most of his remaining resources to clearing the Schelde Estuary.

The Germans had never doubted the importance of the port of Antwerp to the Allied cause. The Germans were well aware of Eisenhower's logistical problems and had accurately predicted that his armies would soon be halted unless they had access to a deep-water port. They knew that Montgomery would eventually capture Antwerp and they were ready with reinforced defensive positions around the Schelde Estuary soon after the port fell to Montgomery's forces in early September.

The Germans also took advantage of delays due to Allied supply problems to reorganize and reinforce their forces along the western front and at the Schelde Estuary. It would take the British and Canadian armies until November 8 (at a cost of 13,000 casualties) to clear the Schelde Estuary of German forces. The first Allied supply ship docked at the port of Antwerp on November 28, 1944.

OPENING MOVES 39

## Chapter Two

# THE GERMAN ATTACK AND AMERICAN REACTION

With enemy armies camped on Germany's doorsteps, and with Germany under constant aerial attack, even Hitler realized by late 1944 that the war could not continue indefinitely. At the highest level of Germany's military and civilian leadership, it was accepted that there remained only enough supplies to keep the ground forces going for six more months. Any estimates for a longer lease on life were deemed to be unrealistic. The German economy was collapsing as the country's railroad and communication systems were breaking down under a rain of Allied high explosive bombs. The lack of fuel had already grounded much of the German Air Force (Luftwaffe) and would soon immobilize the mechanized elements of the German Army (Heer) and the Waffen SS.

Reflecting the long tradition within the German military that the best defense is a good offense, Hitler refused to wait for the Allied armies to begin their final assault on Germany. Having been a political gambler, and knowing that time was fast running out for himself and his "Thousand Year" Third Reich, Hitler was determined to launch one last massive offensive operation before it was too late.

Beginning in late August, Hitler and his senior staff tried to decide if it would be better to launch a large offensive operation on the western or eastern front. After much thought, it was decided that the Soviet Union's apparently unlimited manpower reserves and the large size of the country would frustrate any German efforts to gain a strategic decision in the East.

General Alfred Jodl, a member of Hitler's senior headquarters staff, stated to his Allied captors after the war that the attack had to be launched "in the west because the Russians had so many troops that even if we had succeeded in destroying 30 divisions, it would have made no difference. On the other hand, if we destroyed 30 divisions in the west, it would amount to more than one-third of the whole invasion army." Actually this would have been almost half of Eisenhower's divisions in Europe in late 1944.

Hitler, who was aware of the bickering between the senior British and American

*Above and Opposite:* In early August 1944, even before Hitler announced his intentions for a counteroffensive against the Western Allies, he ordered that the western front be given priority on tanks coming off the assembly line, as well as new artillery and assault gun (tank destroyer) production. Only 485 of these well-known German Tiger II heavy tanks were built before the war ended. *British Army Tank Museum*

THE GERMAN ATTACK AND AMERICAN REACTION 41

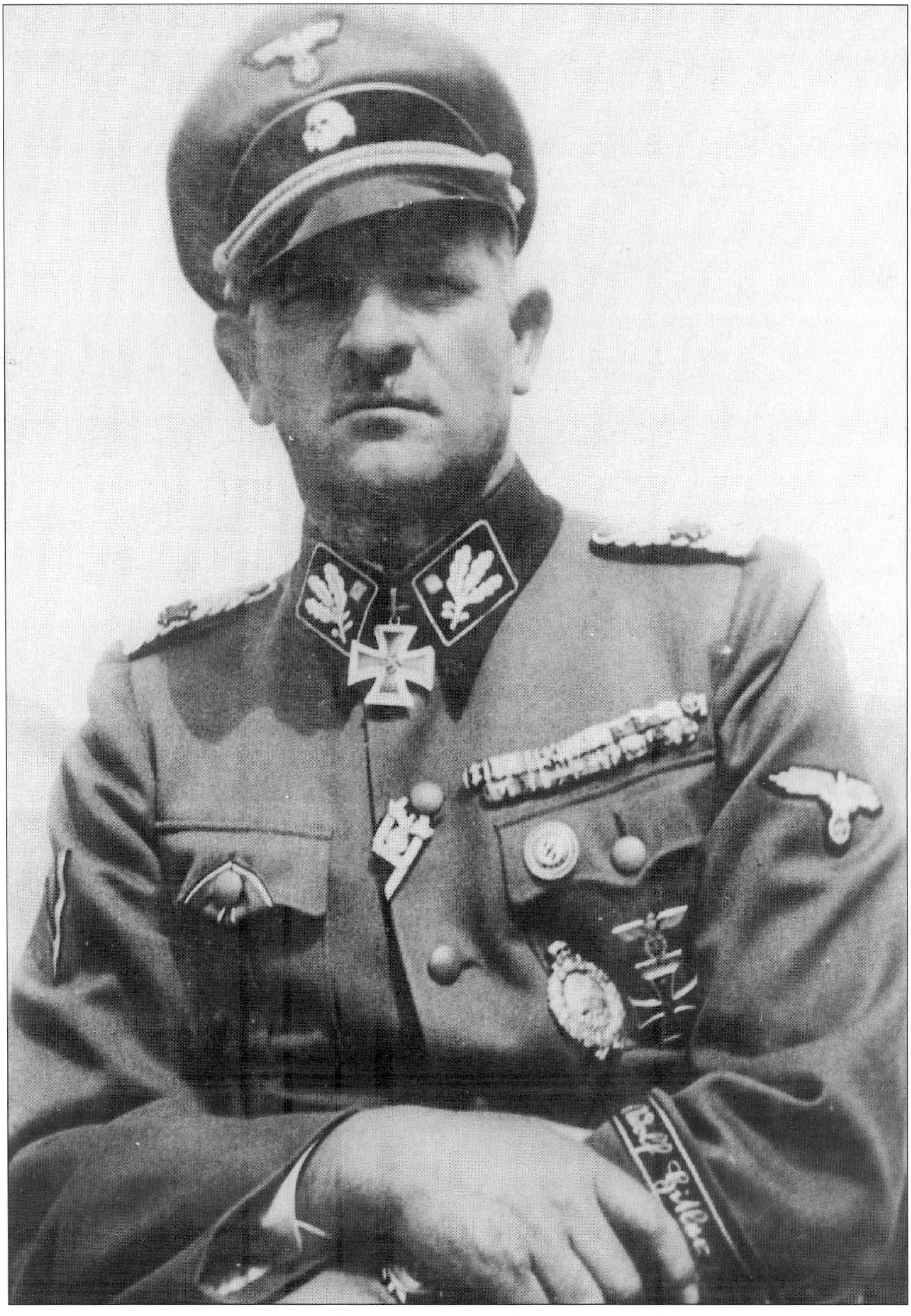

In order to build up the forces needed for the planned counteroffensive, Hitler had given strict orders to his senior generals that divisions assigned to it could not be used for other purposes. The first test of this decree came on November 8, 1944, when Patton, here giving a pep talk to a small group of soldiers, opened a two-corps attack south of the Ardennes, in the French province of Lorraine. *Patton Museum*

military leaders, incorrectly believed that a German victory on the western front would create a serious rift between the respective allies. He also felt that if things played out the way he anticipated, public opinion, especially in the United States, would demand a withdrawal of American forces from Europe. This consideration led Hitler to decide in September 1944 to mount a large offensive operation on the western front instead of the eastern front. This decision coincided with Hitler's firm conviction that Germany's fate would be decided on the western front.

Hitler's grand plan called for the German Army and Waffen SS panzer and infantry divisions to split the two main Allied armies apart at their weakest point, in the Ardennes's sector of Hodges' American First Army. If that objective could be accomplished, Hitler optimistically hoped this would allow his forces to drive on to the main Allied supply port of Antwerp, less than 100 air miles away. In the process, the German forces would cut off Montgomery's 21st Army Group from its supply base and force it to evacuate the continent. Failing that, at least it would put Hitler in a good position to sign separate peace agreements with the Allies, avoiding the disastrous

Early on in his planning for the Ardennes counteroffensive, Hitler decided that the main thrust of the operation would be borne by the Waffen SS panzer divisions already fighting the Allies. To refit them for the coming counteroffensive, Hitler ordered them out of the line on September 13, 1944. Once withdrawn to rest areas inside of Germany, the divisions were turned over to the Sixth Panzer Army, commanded by General Joseph (Sepp) Dietrich. *National Archives*

### The Battle of the Bulge: German Objectives

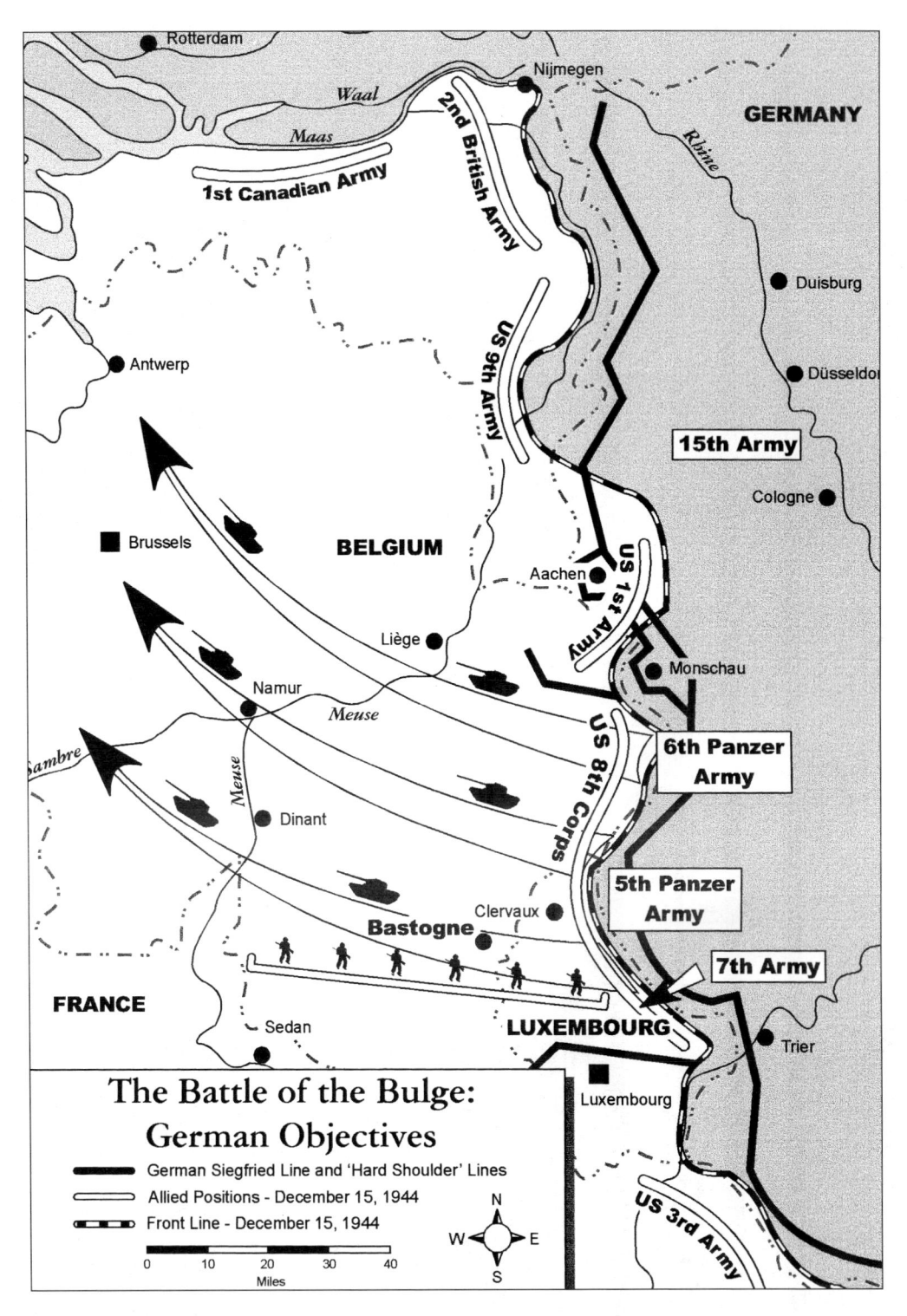

- German Siegfried Line and 'Hard Shoulder' Lines
- Allied Positions - December 15, 1944
- Front Line - December 15, 1944

and humiliating unconditional surrender American President Franklin D. Roosevelt had spelled out in early 1944.

Once Hitler had made up his mind regarding the direction of his last great offensive, his headquarters staff had to figure out how to implement his plan. Important factors they had to bear in mind included Hitler's strategic objectives, available German forces (amounting to about 30 divisions), and Allied strength and capabilities. The key trump card held by the Allies was their absolute control of the air over all of western Europe. To work around this problem, Hitler's staff decided that they would need at least 10 days of bad weather to keep Allied planes grounded during the initial phase

44 PATTON AND THE BATTLE OF THE BULGE

of the Ardennes counteroffensive.

In preparation for his planned Ardennes counteroffensive, Hitler recalled the 67-year-old Field Marshal Gerd von Rundstedt into service in September 1944. As the senior active service officer of the German Army, having joined the Imperial army of the Kaiser in 1892, Rundstedt commanded a great deal of respect and prestige within the officer corps of the army. Hitler appointed Rundstedt commander in chief of the western forces.

As head of OB West once more, Rundstedt was given command of the B, G, and H army groups. These three army groups were responsible for all ground operations in western Germany, Belgium, Holland, and France. Despite his title as Commander in Chief, OB West, Rundstedt was in effect a mere figurehead with little or no power. Hitler had lost what little trust he had in the majority of senior officers of the German Army after the abortive July 1944 plot by a small group of army officers to assassinate him, and from that point on, he virtually took over the daily direction of the German battlefronts.

Two American soldiers examine a trailer-mounted German rocket launcher, captured in Patton's Third Army offensive in Lorraine in November 1944. As a result of Patton's attack, two German panzer divisions scheduled for use in Hitler's Ardennes counteroffensive never made it into that fray. A third panzer division, the Panzer Lehr, limped back to its assembly area much reduced in strength and with badly shaken morale. *National Archives*

American armored infantry troops ride in their lightly armored M-3 half-track in the Ardennes region in late 1944. Weak Allied forces defending the Ardennes attracted Hitler's interest. He and his generals knew that the success of the planned counteroffensive would depend on surprise and reaching their objectives as quickly as possible. *National Archives*

THE GERMAN ATTACK AND AMERICAN REACTION 45

A very impatient Hitler was forced by unpleasant logistical realities to postpone his Ardennes counteroffensive until December 16. Even this additional delay failed to provide enough time for all the preparations needed to launch an operation in the size and scope that Hitler demanded. The German 170-millimeter howitzer was the standard heavy howitzer in the German Army, capable of hurling a 249-pound high-explosive round out to a range of 18,340 yards. *Aberdeen Proving Grounds Museum*

The much inflated order of battle originally envisioned by Hitler for his Ardennes counteroffensive called for the movement and assembly of 4 armies, 11 corps, 38 divisions, 9 artillery corps, and 7 rocket brigades, plus service and support troops. By the beginning of December 1944, the order of battle had shrunk to about 30 divisions divided among 3 armies. American soldiers pose on the very long barrel of a captured German railroad gun. *National Archives*

Hitler was well read in military matters and had convinced himself that he knew more about military strategy than his senior generals. What he lacked was an appreciation of the extensive planning and preparation needed to implement his grandiose ideas, skills that were second nature for the professionally trained senior officers of the German Army.

When Rundstedt became head of OB West, he took over from Field Marshal Wolther Model, who stepped down to become commander of Army Group B. In reality, Model would remain the senior officer in charge of the

Once Luettwitz returned to his XLVII Corps headquarters, he issued instructions to his subordinates: "Bastogne must be captured, if necessary from the rear. Otherwise it will be an abscess in the route of advance and tie up too many forces. Bastogne is to be mopped up first, then the bulk of the corps continues its advance." Two somewhat tired looking American soldiers share a break together in Bastogne. *National Archives*

Specifically, the XLVII Panzer Corps was to cross the Our River on a wide front, take Bastogne, and move to and cross the Meuse River south of Namur. This knocked-out German self-propelled 150-millimeter howitzer was mounted on the armored chassis of a Mark IV medium tank. *Patton Museum*

The Germans expected that the advance to the Meuse would not be delayed by any attack on Bastogne, because both would be accomplished simultaneously. This German 128-millimeter antiaircraft gun was mounted on a specially modified railroad flat car. *Aberdeen Proving Grounds Museum*

majority of preparations for Hitler's Ardennes counteroffensive. Model was nicknamed "the Fuehrer's fireman" for his ability to repeatedly snatch victory from the jaws of defeat on the eastern front.

As one of the few senior German Army officers whom Hitler still trusted to make an all-out effort when ordered, Model was Hitler's first choice to help organize and lead the Ardennes counteroffensive. Rundstedt, on the other hand, knew that he was only a figurehead and divorced himself from most of the operation. Despite Hitler's faith in Model's ability to carry out his plans, Model, like Rundstedt, had little hope for the success of Hitler's Ardennes counteroffensive.

Due to the respect that the Allied senior military leaders had for Rundstedt's abilities, and their lack of understanding about the Byzantine nature of Hitler's overall strategy, the Ardennes counteroffensive was commonly referred to as the "Rundstedt Offensive" during the war and for a long time afterward. Only when Allied historians had a chance to interview the senior German officers who survived the war, did they begin to understand the true nature of command arrangements at Hitler's headquarters. In an Allied prison after the war, Rundstedt would tell his captors, "The Ardennes counteroffensive bore my name quite wrongly. I had nothing to with it. It was ordered from above down to the smallest detail."

Despite Rundstedt's strong belief that Hitler's Ardennes counteroffensive was doomed from the start, he and his staff wasted no time in pulling together all available resources to strengthen the western borders of Germany. It would not be an easy task. During the battle for France, the Germans lost almost a half-million men, the equivalent of 43 divisions. Material losses were put at 3,500 artillery pieces and antitank guns, thousands of wheeled vehicles, and at least 1,500 tanks.

As commander of Army Group B, Field Marshal Model had three field armies assigned to him by Hitler to carry out his Ardennes counteroffensive. They included the Sixth and Fifth Panzer Armies and the Seventh Army. The three armies were deployed in a line abreast formation (decided by Hitler, not Model) facing the American-held Ardennes in Belgium and Luxembourg.

The first assault wave of the Sixth Panzer Army consisted of the 1st SS Panzer corps, consisting of two armored and three infantry divisions, and the LXVII Corps with two infantry divisions. As the German field army nearest Antwerp, and the largest and most powerful of the three German armies, Hitler assigned to it the main effort during the Ardennes counteroffensive.

The plan was to penetrate the American lines in the Ardennes, so the five infantry divisions of the Sixth Panzer Army could combine with the two panzer divisions of the I SS Panzer Corps. The combined forces would then form a defensive shoulder north of the town of Monschau and head westward across the Meuse to Antwerp.

At the Meuse, backup support would come from two panzer divisions of the II SS Panzer Corps. In total, the four panzer divisions assigned to the Sixth Panzer Army had roughly 500 tanks, including 90 of the fearsome Tiger tanks, armed with the dreaded 88-millimeter high-velocity guns.

Hitler appointed an old crony, Generaloberst der Waffen SS Joseph Dietrich (Sepp), commander of the Sixth Panzer Army. During World War I, Dietrich had served as an enlisted man in the small German tank forces, rising eventually to the rank of sergeant. As

Many senior German officers aware of the Hitler's Ardennes counteroffensive doubted whether the offensive would succeed. The Germans had to achieve surprise, and the powerful Allied air forces somehow had to be neutralized. To accomplish this goal, Hitler would have to deliver both sufficient quantities of fuel and the 3,000 German aircraft he had promised on December 11, 1944, for the operation. One of his aircraft, a German Me-109 fighter plane, landed in an irrigation ditch. *National Archives*

# The Battle of the Bulge

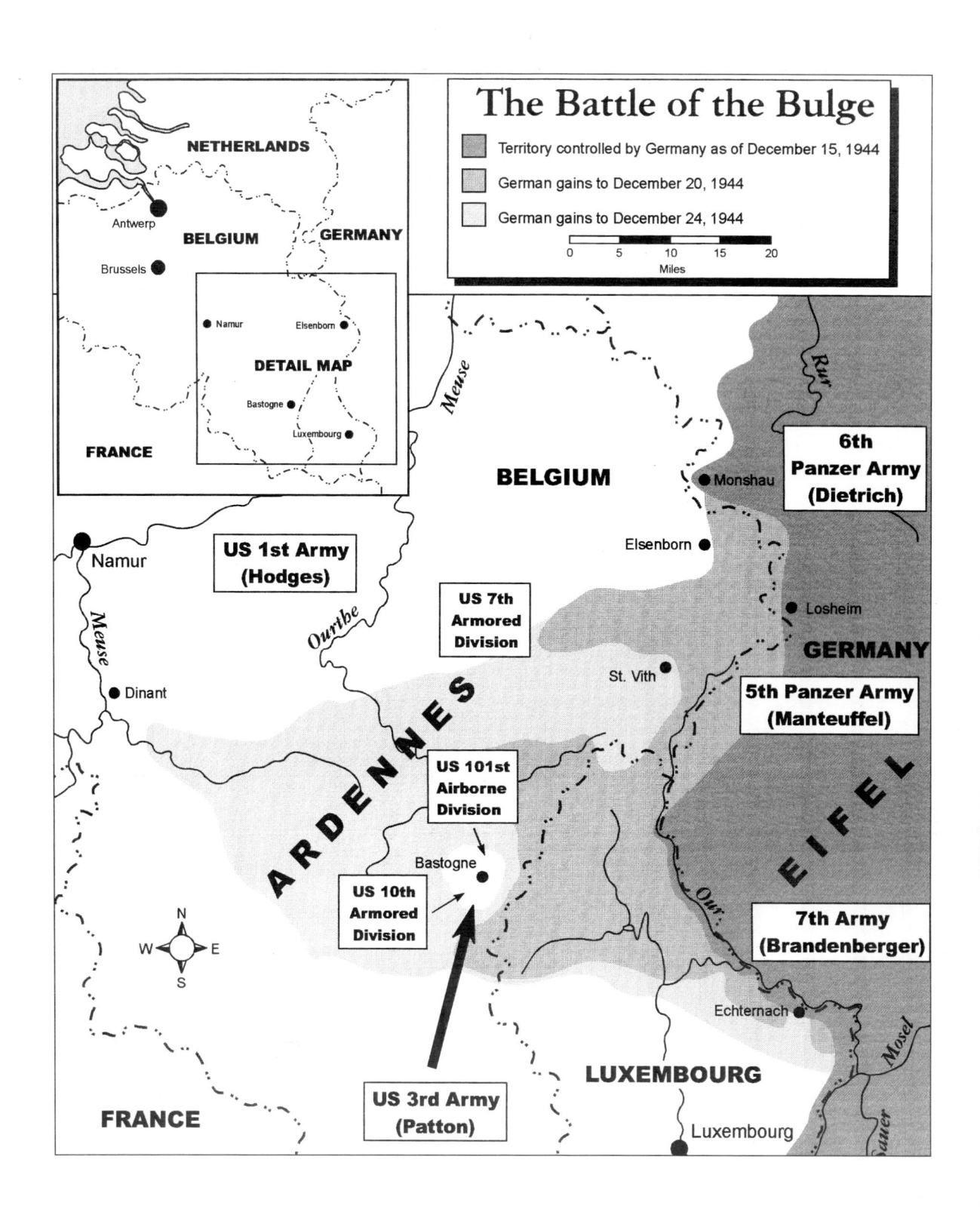

- Territory controlled by Germany as of December 15, 1944
- German gains to December 20, 1944
- German gains to December 24, 1944

0  5  10  15  20
Miles

**NETHERLANDS**
Antwerp
**BELGIUM**
Brussels
**GERMANY**
Namur • Elsenborn
DETAIL MAP
Bastogne
Luxembourg
**FRANCE**

Meuse

**BELGIUM**

Namur

**US 1st Army (Hodges)**

Ourthe

**US 7th Armored Division**

Meuse

Dinant

**ARDENNES**

St. Vith

Monshau

**6th Panzer Army (Dietrich)**

Elsenborn

Losheim

**GERMANY**

**5th Panzer Army (Manteuffel)**

**EIFEL**

**US 101st Airborne Division**

Bastogne

**US 10th Armored Division**

Our

**7th Army (Brandenberger)**

Echternach

Mosel

**LUXEMBOURG**

Luxembourg

Sauer

**US 3rd Army (Patton)**

**FRANCE**

an early member of the Nazi Party, he played an important role in the creation of the Waffen SS. Due to Dietrich's close relationship with Hitler, he quickly rose to the top ranks of the Waffen SS.

## Manteuffel's Fifth Panzer Army

To the left of the Sixth Panzer Army, Hitler deployed the Fifth Panzer Army under the very capable command of Lieutenant General *(General der Panzertruppen)* Baron Hasso-Eccard von Manteuffel. His peers called Manteuffel "the Panzer General" for his successes with armored formations in North Africa and Russia. Many senior Allied military commanders regarded Manteuffel as the "Patton" of the German Army.

After the war Manteuffel described his role in Hitler's Ardennes counteroffensive. "My army was to advance along a more curving line (than the Sixth Panzer Army), cross the Meuse between Namur and Dinant, and push toward Brussels to cover the flank." Manteuffel's Fifth Panzer Army was also assigned the job of protecting the rear of Dietrich's Sixth Panzer Army from counterattack by Allied forces.

Manteuffel's Fifth Panzer Army was the second-strongest of the three armies under Model's control, with three panzer corps deployed for the first assault wave. The Fifth Panzer Army consisted of the XLVII (two panzer divisions and one infantry division), the

Hitler's selection of December 16, 1944, as the beginning of the Ardennes counteroffensive concerned the senior German military leadership. The number of soldiers available for the operation had steadily decreased, most units had not been rested, and all units were suffering from significant shortages of organic weapons, tanks, trucks, spare parts, ammunition, and fuel. An American soldier examines an abandoned German eight-wheel armored car mounting a short-barrel 75-millimeter infantry support howitzer in an open-topped mount. *National Archives*

The XLVII Panzer Corps consisted of the 2nd Panzer Division, Panzer Lehr Division, and the 26th Volksgrenadier Division, all reinforced by one mortar brigade, one artillery corps, and the 600th Army Engineer Battalion, for bridging purposes. None was at full strength. This tank is the command and control version of the German Panther medium tank, fitted with extra radios, as evident by the additional antenna seen on the rear deck of the vehicle. *Frank Schulz collection*

LVIII (one panzer and one infantry division), and the LXVI (with two infantry divisions). The Fifth Panzer Army also had two panzer divisions in reserve.

The mission of Manteuffel's XLVII Panzer Corps was to cross the Our River and seize the important road center of Bastogne, which lay only 19 air miles west of the Fifth Panzer Army's jumping-off positions. Once Bastogne was under German control, the XLVII Corps was to cross the Ourthe and head for the Meuse, crossing south of the Belgian town of Namur.

The XLVII Corps was under the command of General der Panzertruppen Heinrich von Luettwitz. Three divisions made up his corps, the 2nd Panzer Division, the Panzer Lehr (demonstration) Division, and the 26th Volksgrenadier (infantry) Division. It would fall to the 26th, under the command of Generalleutnant Heinz Kokott, to quickly take Bastogne, with or without armor support. The two panzer divisions of the XLVII Corps would reach Bastogne before the 26th Volksgrenadier Division, but had orders to bypass it and continue on to the Meuse.

The Fifth Army's operational plan called for crossing the Meuse by the fourth day of the Ardennes counteroffensive. As it turned out, the 2nd Panzer Division would advance to within 6 miles of the Meuse by December 23, before being stopped by the American 2nd Armored Division at the small Belgian town of Celles. The plan called for the 26th Volksgrenadier Division to capture Bastogne on the second day of the Ardennes counteroffensive. Luettwitz, the corps commander, felt that the

52  PATTON AND THE BATTLE OF THE BULGE

timetable set by his superiors was unrealistic and was doomed to fail.

Prior to the Ardennes counteroffensive, the 26th Volksgrenadier Division had served only on the eastern front, where it saw heavy combat and took stiff losses. Reorganized for its new role on the western front, the unit was considered the best infantry division taking part in the Ardennes counteroffensive.

Typical of the majority of German infantry divisions throughout World War II, the 26th Volksgrenadier Division had little or no motorized transport for its men. Troops generally moved around the battlefield on foot. Heavier equipment was pulled into action by a collection of over 5,000 horses. In contrast, a typical American infantry division had over 2,000 vehicles.

For added support, Manteuffel attached the heavily reinforced motorized reconnaissance battalion of the Panzer Lehr Division to the nonmotorized reconnaissance battalion of the 26th Volksgrenadier Division. Additional support for the three divisions of Luettwitz's corps came from an assortment of werfer (rocket), artillery, engineer, and flak (antiaircraft) units.

Rundstedt had done his best to convince Hitler that Manteuffel and his Fifth Panzer Army would be a better choice than Dietrich's Sixth Panzer Army to lead the main thrust in the upcoming Ardennes counteroffensive. This change in roles would have required the two panzer armies to switch positions. Hitler firmly rejected this suggestion and told Rundstedt that his plans were firmly locked in place.

On the morning of December 16, 1944, the Germans launched their counteroffensive, and gained surprise and immediate local successes in all sectors. In the American VIII Corps sector alone, 25 German divisions were attacking. Major General Troy H. Middleton, in the rear seat of a command car with Patton, commanded VIII Corps, which had the misfortune of being directly astride the main avenue of advance of the Fifth Panzer Army. *Patton Museum*

# AMERICAN ARMORED DIVISION ORGANIZATION

By late 1944, the majority of American armored divisions in Europe consisted of three battalions of tanks and three battalions of armored infantry. Each battalion of an armored division was a self-contained unit with organic tactical and essential administrative elements.

An armored division tank battalion of 1944 had a small headquarters (HQ) company, three medium tank companies of 17 tanks each, and a single light tank company with 17 tanks. A service company kept the battalion's tanks in running condition.

The infantry battalions of a 1944 armored division had five companies: a headquarters company, three rifle companies, and a service company. Each of the three rifle companies consisted of 251 soldiers riding into action in 20 open-topped, lightly armored M3 half-tracks.

Antitank protection for each rifle company came from either the well-known bazooka fitted to each half-track or from three towed 57-millimeter antitank guns. The HQ company of an armored infantry battalion contained a reconnaissance, mortar, and assault gun platoon with a maintenance section to support the entire battalion.

Each armored artillery battalion within a wartime armored division had 18 self-propelled 105-millimeter howitzers. These fully tracked open-topped, self-propelled carriages (mounts) carried the 105-millimeter howitzer into action and were designated by the U.S. Army as either the M7 or M7B1.

To supplement the capabilities of its armored divisions in northwest Europe, the U.S. Army normally attached additional units (from the corps or field army level) on a semipermanent basis. These extra units typically consisted of a tank destroyer battalion, antiaircraft battalion, a battalion of 155-millimeter self-propelled guns, and various supply and engineer companies.

The general in charge of an American armored division in World War II exercised command and control over the fighting battalions of his division through three task force headquarters designated Combat Command A (CCA), Combat Command B (CCB) and Reserve Combat Command (CCR). In theory, these tactical commands possessed no organic fighting troops of their own, but were allotted the combat and service assets required to accomplish their individual missions. This meant, depending on the mission, that a CC could have anywhere between two and six battalions assigned to it.

Many armored division commanders in World War II chose to overlook accepted practice and created combat commands of fixed composition. Typically, this resulted in some armored divisions giving each CC an equal number of tank, infantry, and artillery battalions. This type of organization within a CC was referred to as a "balanced" formation.

Some armored division commanders in Europe favored the "unbalanced" type of combat command in which CCs were organized according to the type of weapon and equipment of the battalions assigned to them. Consequently, one CC would have most of the infantry battalions, and the other CC would be composed mostly of tanks. As a standard operating practice in Europe, both the balanced and the unbalanced form of CCs would have other units such as engineers, reconnaissance, antiaircraft, tank destroyer, and supply support attached.

Patton's elite Fourth Armored Division was a strong believer in never assigning battalions to a CC on a fixed basis, preferring instead to retain a high degree of flexibility in its task organization.

The U.S. Army originally envisioned that the CCR of an armored division was to be employed strictly in reserve to act as a pool for all combat elements not assigned to CCs. However, some armored division commanders, when hard-pressed by combat conditions, would upgrade their CCRs into full-fledged CCs by assigning additional headquarters personnel to control them.

The CCA and CCB headquarters of an armored division each had about 12 officers and 80 enlisted men. Reflecting its intended role as strictly a nontactical reserve, a CCR typically had only three officers and five enlisted men in its headquarters. If the CCR headquarters was contemplated for use as a CC, it had to obtain additional staff officers from the division HQ.

Depending on the mission, the CCs of an armored division could be subdivided into smaller task forces if required. Task forces normally consisted of mixed companies of armor and armored infantry. They were typically named after the officer in command of the task force.

One level down from the task forces were the small "teams." They consisted of a mixed company of armor and armored infantry. For example, a platoon of five tanks and a platoon of 40 armored infantrymen could act as a team. Teams were designated by single capital letter such as Team A, B, or C.

As events unfolded during the Battle of the Bulge, it was Manteuffel's Fifth Panzer Army that made the greatest German penetration into Allied territory. As early as December 20, the lack of progress by Dietrich's Sixth Panzer Army caused Model to switch his armored reserves to Manteuffel's Fifth Panzer Army. Manteuffel's panzer divisions would

Middleton's VIII Corps, which formed the southern flank of the American First Army, occupied an 88-mile front extended from Losheim, Germany, north through eastern Belgium and Luxembourg to where the Our River crosses the Franco-German border. American soldiers advance past two destroyed German turretless tank destroyers designated as the Jagdpanzer 38 Hetzer. The vehicle was armed with a high-velocity 75-millimeter antitank gun. *British Army Tank Museum*

Middleton's corps had been assigned the Ardennes region because Eisenhower and Bradley considered it a relatively quiet sector. There, new divisions could receive a safe break-in period before being introduced into full-scale combat operations, and battle-weary ones could rest and reconstitute for future operations. Patton was against this arrangement from the beginning, since he felt it would invite a German attack. American soldiers make use of a captured German 105-millimeter field howitzer to fire at its former owners. *National Archives*

THE GERMAN ATTACK AND AMERICAN REACTION   55

now spearhead the main thrust of Hitler's doomed Ardennes counteroffensive.

Like his superiors, Manteuffel had little confidence in the success of Hitler's Ardennes counteroffensive. In a postwar interview with his Allied captors, Manteuffel stated some of the reasons that he felt the operation was doomed from the beginning:

"The number of forces launching the attack on 15 December was not in proportion to the objective (Antwerp), which had been placed too far ahead. The operation lacked the necessary personnel and material for the speedy and powerful exploitation of a successful breakthrough. There were not enough forces from which units could be brought up to eliminate pockets of resistance not taken, but partially by-passed, during the initial assault, from which to feed the attack from the rear. Furthermore, there were not enough men to protect the flanks of the spearhead, unless the units planned for the thrust to the Meuse were employed. The supreme command, therefore, insisted upon a quick defeat of the enemy on the front attack to counterbalance the disadvantage of insufficient depth; also by the speed of the advance, the forming of an enemy defense line on the Meuse was to be prevented."

As discussed before, the LVIII Panzer Corps of Manteuffel's Fifth Panzer Army was given the assignment of crossing the Our River and then racing to the Meuse to create a bridgehead north of the XLVII Panzer Corps at the town of Namur. The infantry divisions of the LXVI Panzer Corps were to take the small Belgian road center of St. Vith and then follow the LVIII Panzer Corps on to the Meuse.

In a postwar interview, Manteuffel stated that he had hoped that the LXVI Corps could take St. Vith on the first day of the attack.

Headquarters for Middleton's VIII Corps was located in Bastogne. The area around the town was characterized by rugged hills, high plateaus, deep-cut valleys, and restricted road nets. Bastogne itself was the center for seven roads and a railroad. Both American and German commanders understood the significance of Bastogne's location and would plan their future operations around it. The American crew of a .50-caliber M-2 machine gun (air-cooled) is preparing its weapon for use. *National Archives*

As the German counteroffensive struck Middleton's VIII Corps, the only reserves he had available consisted of a single CC from the 9th Armored Division and four battalions of combat engineers, the 44th, 35th, 168th, and 150th. Middleton would put the engineers in the line as infantry to fight not only in the defense of Bastogne, but also St. Vith and Wiltz. American soldiers carry antitank mines into a snow-covered Ardennes meadow. *National Archives*

Instead, the Germans had the misfortune of running into Combat Command "B" (CCB) of the 7th Armored Division, which was defending the road center. The commander of CCB was Brigadier General Bruce C. Clark, who had just been transferred in from Patton's elite Fourth Armored Division. Clark was assisted in the defense of St. Vith by an assortment of retreating American units that came through the town and were pressed into its defense.

Between December 16 and December 23, the 10,000 American defenders of St. Vith would ward off countless attacks by over 87,000 soldiers of Manteuffel's Fifth Panzer Army. Engagements at St. Vith are not as well known as the defense of Bastogne by the 101st Airborne Division, but the key delaying action fought at St. Vith would effectively derail the critical German timeline that was so crucial for the overall success of Hitler's Ardennes counteroffensive. Many historians consider the battle for St. Vith, and not the battle for Bastogne, as the true turning point in the Battle of the Bulge.

### Brandenberger's Seventh Army
On the left flank of Manteuffel's Fifth Panzer Army was the Seventh Army, under the com-

Confusion and disorganization marked the American units caught in the path of Hitler's counteroffensive. The Germans advanced steadily, but not as rapidly as they had hoped. The roads used by the Germans quickly became overcrowded, and small pockets of determined resistance waged by American infantry and armored units slowed, but did not stop the German advance. Pictured guarding possible avenues of approach are these American 57-mm antitank guns. It was the US Army's standard light antitank gun in World War II. *National Archives*

mand of General der Panzertruppen Erich Brandenberger. Brandenberger was not as well known as Hitler's good friend Sepp Dietrich or the highly regarded Manteuffel, but he was an experienced officer with a solid record of achievements fighting the Russians.

Brandenberger's Seventh Army was given only a secondary role in Hitler's great Ardennes counteroffensive. The Seventh Army had orders to form a defensive line on the angle formed by the Semois and the Meuse Rivers. The intent of the defensive line was to protect the exposed southern flank of the Fifth Panzer Army from a counterattack by Patton's Third Army, located roughly 100 miles south of Bastogne.

Brandenberger calculated that he would need at least six infantry divisions and from one or two panzer divisions to successfully accomplish its defensive mission, within the context of Hitler's Ardennes counteroffensive. The Seventh Army commander also requested the attachment of additional artillery, werfer (rocket launchers), and bridge engineering units to his command.

For numerous reasons, Hitler restricted Brandenberger's Seventh Army to the bare minimum of only five infantry divisions. They included four volksgrenadier divisions and the Luftwaffe 5th Parachute Division. Three of the volksgrenadier divisions, the 212th, 276th, and 340th, came under the operational control of the LXXX Corps, commanded by Generalder Infanterie Franz Beyer. The remaining volksgrenadier division (the 352nd) and the 5th Parachute Division came under the operational control of the LXXXV Corps, commanded by General Bapist Kneiss. The Seventh Army had the LIII Corps, consisting of two volksgrenadier divisions, in reserve.

Based on the military resources assigned to him, Brandenberger decided to have the three volksgrenadier divisions of the LXXX Corps cross the Our River as far forward as Luxembourg. Once they reached their assigned objectives, the LXXX Corps was ordered to establish a defensive line to delay any enemy advance to the north or northeast through Luxembourg.

## Bastogne Is Surrounded

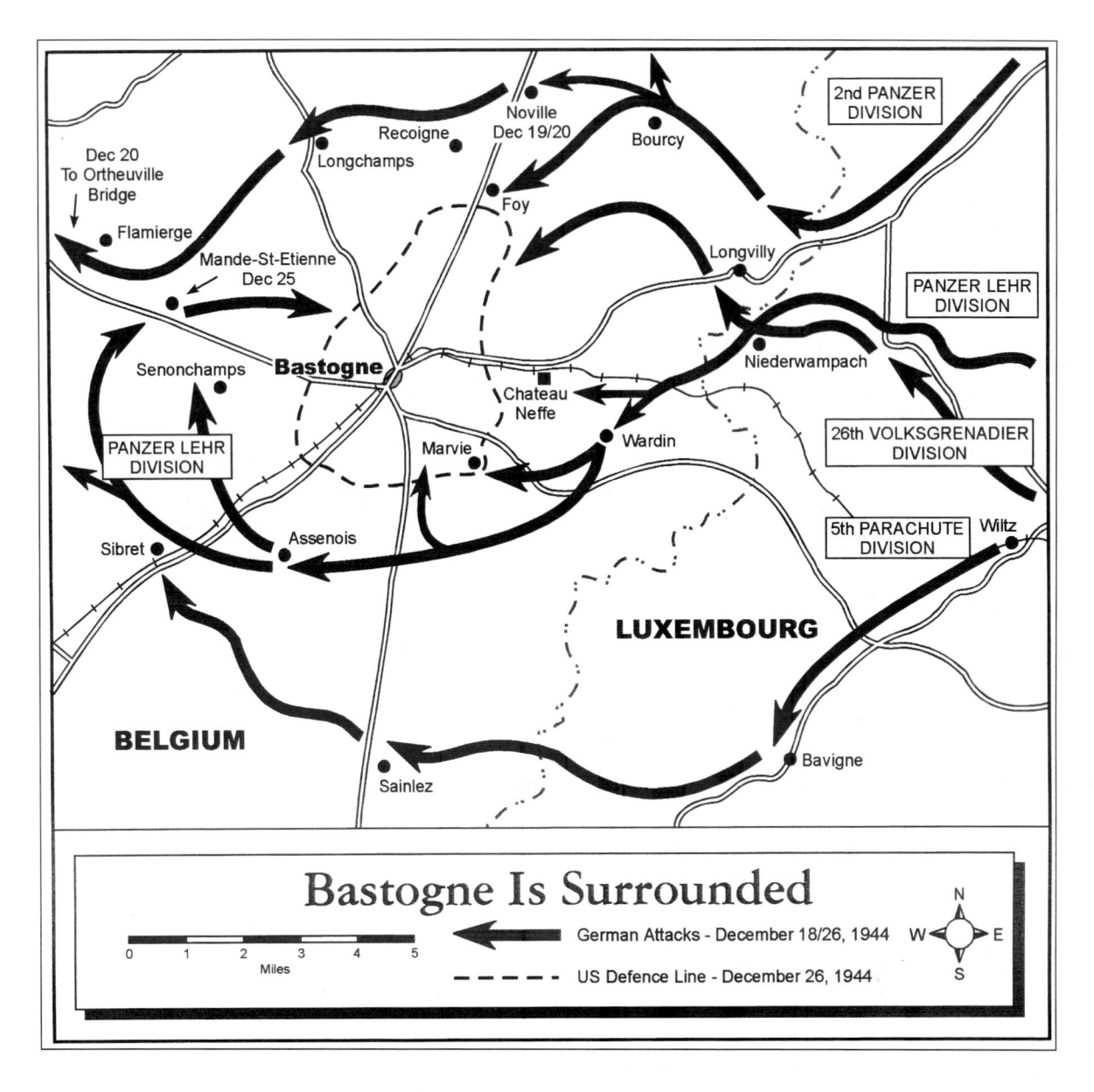

German Attacks - December 18/26, 1944
US Defence Line - December 26, 1944

The two divisions of the LXXXV Corps were ordered to cross the Our River and advance westward in step with the south flank of Manteuffel's Fifth Panzer Army. As the Fifth Panzer Army passed through (or around) Bastogne, the 5th Parachute Division would deploy in a defensive line to the south of the town. The 352nd Volksgrenadier Division would continue marching until it reached the Semois River, where it would establish a defensive line to deny the enemy a crossing point.

Manteuffel was greatly concerned by the apparent weakness of Brandenberger's forces. He feared the infantry formations of the Seventh Army would be unable to keep up with his rapidly moving panzer divisions on their way to Bastogne. In spite of Manteuffel's strong request, Hitler refused to provide the Seventh Army with a mechanized infantry division.

There were two good reasons for Hitler's refusal. First, Patton's offensive operations in the French province of Lorraine during November and early December of 1944 had forced the German senior military leadership to delay the movement of many of its best divisions to the strategic reserve that was being gathered for use in the upcoming Ardennes counteroffensive. The high German losses suffered during the fighting in Lorraine also allowed the bulk of Patton's Third Army to easily break contact in that sector when it counterattacked to the north at the

60   PATTON AND THE BATTLE OF THE BULGE

Eisenhower, conferring here with Bradley, soon realized that Bastogne was threatened, and that reserves were needed immediately. Accordingly, on December 17, 1944, the 101st Airborne Division, then in France, was alerted to move to the vicinity of Bastogne. Unlike Eisenhower, Bradley completely failed to grasp the seriousness of Hitler's counteroffensive in the Ardennes at the beginning. *National Archives*

Bastogne, if held, could interrupt lines of communication as the Germans continued their attack westward. In the meanwhile, VIII Corps' defenses were crumbling, and the Germans, who averaged 4 to 8 miles advance on the first day, were already within 11 miles of Bastogne. Time had become a critical factor. The race was on to see which side could reach Bastogne in force first. Moving along a snow-covered Ardennes road is this American M-18 tank destroyer. *National Archives*

southern flank of the German penetration in the Ardennes.

The second reason for Hitler's refusal to reinforce Brandenberger's Seventh Army was his firm conviction that it would take the Allies a great deal of time before they could organize and launch strong counterattacks. Hitler also believed that if the Allies did launch a major counterattack, it would more than likely be aimed at the German forces attempting to reach the Meuse. He felt that it was unlikely that the Seventh Army would be attacked at the southern flank of the Fifth Panzer.

Brandenberger and his Seventh Army staff disagreed with Hitler on this point. In a post-war prison interview, Brandenberger explained his reasoning to his Allied captors:

"Since it was highly probable that the Franco-Belgian area contained no large reserves, the possibility had to be considered that all available enemy troops in the area of Metz and perhaps also in the sector opposite Army Group G would be brought up for offensive action against the southern flank of the attacking German armies. And for that, the roads leading north through Luxembourg and Arlon would be considered first. The Seventh Army estimated that strong enemy forces would arrive in the Arlon area north of Luxembourg not earlier than the fourth day of the attack. The fact that these forces would probably be commanded by General Patton made it quite likely that the enemy would direct a heavy punch against the deep flank of the German forces scheduled to be in the vicinity of

Bastogne. In the Battle of France, Patton had given proof of his extraordinary skill in armored warfare, which he conducted according to the fundamental German conception."

## The Allied Reaction

In the early morning hours of December 16, 1944, the full force of Hitler's Ardennes counteroffensive struck Hodges' First Army units deployed in the Ardennes. Hitler's strong emphasis on secrecy and trickery in conjunction with poor intelligence work on the Allied side, resulted in the Germans achieving almost complete tactical surprise over the Americans.

A German newspaper article published on December 19 described the opening stage of the Ardennes attack:

"The German offensive in the west stands at the forefront of all events. Powerful German formations have launched a major attack on the western front. The initial concentration before the German attack, which came as a complete surprise to the Americans in spite of the constant superiority of the enemy in the air in the neighborhood of the front, was an unsurpassed masterpiece of German commandership. The German forces advanced over a broad front from the West Wall between Hohes Venn and northern Luxembourg. A short but powerful artillery preparation and the intervention of German fighter and attack planes supported their advance, and our forces overran and broke through the American lines at the first attack."

Major General Troy H. Middleton's overextended three-division VIII Corps occupied the First Army's southern sector where the main German attack was located. A long defensive line and lack of manpower had prevented Middleton from maintaining a mobile reserve to plug any gaps in an emergency. If attacked, Middleton's troops would have to rely on help from outside the Ardennes. Hitler knew this and chose to launch his forces through the Ardennes.

Complicating Middleton's defense mission was the poor condition of his troops. Two of his divisions were still recovering from heavy losses incurred in the previous three months of fighting. The third had no combat experience. (A fourth unit, the 9th Armored Division, had been assigned to VIII Corps, but one of its two combat commands was attached to the neighboring V Corps.)

As the German forces pushed through Middleton's front lines in the Ardennes, the resulting disruption in communications created widespread confusion. Bradley, the 12th Army Group commander did not know about the attack until the afternoon of December 16 as he sat in conference with Eisenhower at his headquarters. Eisenhower's intelligence officer, British Major General Ken Strong, told both men, "The Germans have counterattacked in

Designed to enter combat from the air, either by gliders or parachutes, the 101st Airborne Division had little organic transportation other than jeeps. To move the division the 107 miles to Bastogne, over 300 trucks of various types were rounded up from various sources and pressed into service as troop transports. The vehicles employed to move the parachutists included everything from the U.S. Army's standard 2 1/2 ton trucks, all the way up to 10-ton trucks towing large open-topped trailers. *Michael Green*

As the truck columns carrying the 101st Airborne Division moved through heavy traffic toward Bastogne, CCB of the 10th Armored Division, the 705th Tank Destroyer Battalion, and two battalions of 155-millimeter artillery were ordered to Bastogne to be attached to the 101st. These formations and a replacement pool of stragglers culled from a variety of retreating units would bolster the strength of the 101st Airborne Division during the battle for Bastogne. Pictured in the Ardennes is an American 90-millimeter antiaircraft gun. *Patton Museum*

the Ardennes and scored penetrations at five places on the VIII Corps front." Strong would go on to explain that the attacks had begun early that morning and that the full extent of the attack was still unknown. He did, however, state, "The most dangerous penetration seems to be developing along the V Corps–VIII Corps boundary in the Losheim Gap."

Eisenhower's and Bradley's reactions to Strong's announcement were dramatically different. Bradley regarded the German attack as merely a spoiling attack, aimed at taking the steam out of his own ongoing offensive operations. He also stated his opinion that the attack could be stopped without much difficulty. In contrast, Eisenhower seemed to sense immediately that something far bigger had been set into play. "That's no spoiling attack!" Eisenhower told Bradley.

After studying various maps with Bradley and Strong, Eisenhower directed Bradley to quickly dispatch elements of the 7th and 10th Armored Divisions to the aid of Middleton's hard-pressed VIII Corps. Part of the 7th Armored Division was sent to defend St. Vith. It was detached from Lieutenant General William H. Simpson's Ninth Army located north of the Ardennes. Elements of the 10th Armored Division were redeployed to Bastogne from Patton's Third Army located south of the Ardennes.

While this was Patton's first official notice of the German's Ardennes counteroffensive, he had anticipated the attack and, on December 12, had even directed his staff to make "a study of what the Third Army would do if called upon to counterattack such a breakthrough."

Patton's intuition about the German offensive in the Ardennes area was based on the solid information being collected and analyzed by the head of his intelligence (G-2) section, Colonel Oscar W. Koch. Patton once stated: "Oscar Koch is the best damned intelligence officer in any United States Army Command." During November, Koch identified a number of German units leaving Westphalia (Germany) and the Third Army's front. Koch believed they were regrouping somewhere. On November 23, he wrote in his daily periodic report: "This powerful striking force, with an estimated 500 tanks, is still an untouched strategic reserve held for future employment," and he concluded they might be used for a "coordinated counteroffensive."

Through early December, Koch continued to pursue information on this possible threat. On December 7, he warned of "enemy reserves with large panzer concentrations west of the Rhine in the northern portion of 12th Army Group's zone of advance." Two days later, Koch informally briefed Patton on the possibility of a German attack and their capability to mount it. On the 11th, Koch again warned, "Overall, the initiative still rests with the Allies. But the massive armored force the enemy has built up in reserve gives him the definite capability of launching a spoiling offensive to disrupt Allied plans." Koch's predictions ran counter to most other higher headquarters intelligence units.

While visiting several division headquarters on December 12, Patton decided to place the 6th Armored Division and the 26th Infantry Division in the III Corps near Saarbrilcken. He felt that the enemy would probably attack the VIII

Corps of the First Army, and that he could use the III Corps to attack straight north, west of the Moselle. That day Patton directed his staff to study what the Third Army would do if requested to counterattack a breakthrough to the north of Third Army.

Four days later, during his normal morning meeting and still unaware that the Germans had begun their attack through the Ardennes an hour earlier, Patton was briefed on the German intercepts from the previous evening. They indicated that the German armored formations around Trier, Germany were spreading out and moving to an unknown destination. The Germans had also just gone on radio silence. Patton was now certain that the attack would be through the Ardennes.

He asked General Hobart R. Gay, his chief of staff, and Colonel Halley G. Maddox, his G-3 (operations and plans chief), how they were progressing on the study that he had ordered on December 12. After they updated him, he made his instructions more specific. "I want you, gentlemen, to start making plans for pulling the Third Army out of its eastward attack, changing the direction 90 degrees, moving to Luxembourg, and attacking north."

Patton was not overly surprised by Bradley's phone call on the evening of December 16 asking for the 10th Armored Division to be sent northward. During their daily morning briefing on December 17, Koch reported that

Waiting for the 101st Airborne Division to reach Bastogne, Middleton, the VIII Corps commander, had to find some way to delay the German units heading toward Bastogne at the same time. He therefore dispatched the recently arrived combat command, CCB, to the northeast, east, and southeast of the town with orders to hold their positions at all cost. Such action quickly indicated to the Germans that Bastogne would not be surrendered. The best-armed tank the American Army had in December 1944 was this version of the M-4 Sherman medium tank, armed with a high-velocity 76-millimeter gun. *Patton Museum*

THE GERMAN ATTACK AND AMERICAN REACTION 65

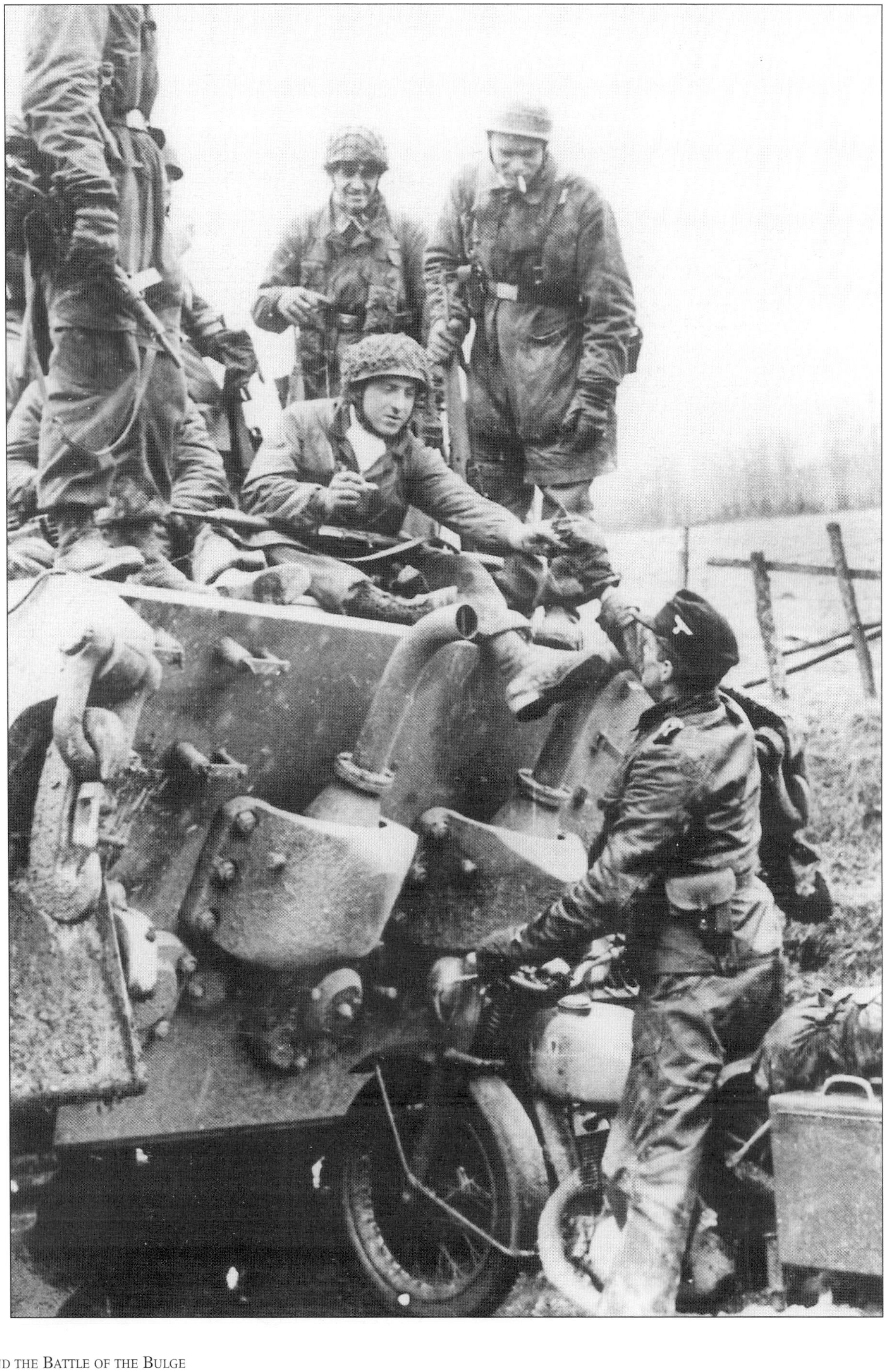

American soldiers armed with a .30-caliber (water-cooled) light machine gun scan the terrain around Bastogne, as the 101st Airborne Division formed its defensive perimeter on the night of December 18. The tide of events had begun to turn. German troops, pressed by their commanders for a faster rate of advance, were near exhaustion. *National Archives*

the Germans were continuing their attack on VIII Corps and that they also appeared to be moving into the area occupied by the Third Army's XX Corps.

Patton considered this new information for a moment, then said,

"One of these is a feint; one is the real thing. If they attack us, I'm ready for them, but I'm inclined to think the party will be up north. VIII Corps has been sitting still—a sure invitation to trouble."

The 101st Airborne Division and its supporting units moved into Bastogne during the night of December 18, just beating a German advance guard unit. A German paratrooper riding on the rear deck of a Tiger II heavy tank gives a cigarette to a Waffen SS motorcycle messenger. *National Archives*

## Third Army Staff

Patton was a strong believer in the importance of a good staff. After the war, he suggested "no one man can conduct an army, but the success of any army depends on the harmonious working of its staff and the magnificent fighting ability of the combat officers and enlisted men. Without this teamwork, war cannot be successfully fought."

During the Battle of the Bulge, Patton's staff pulled off a series of impressive accomplishments that helped turn the tide against the German counteroffensive in the Ardennes. Prior to the campaign, few senior officers shared Patton's enthusiasm for his staff. His staff's performance during the Battle of the Bulge would change many minds. Bradley later cited an example:

## VOLKSGRENADIER DIVISIONS

The term *volksgrenadier* was a late-war honorific title selected by Hitler to appeal to the national and military pride of the German people *(das Volk)*. Due to heavy wartime losses in manpower, Hitler decided in September 1944 to create a new type of infantry division. It would be either newly raised, or based on the rebuilding of older established infantry divisions.

Volksgrenadier divisions typically had a strength of only 10,000 men. This was in sharp contrast to earlier German infantry divisions with 17,000 men and a fairly large complement of organic artillery support. The typical American infantry division of 1944 had a total strength of 14,500 men.

To provide the men needed for his new volksgrenadier divisions, Hitler had put into effect a series of drastic measures. These included reducing the authorized levels of existing infantry divisions and stripping training and other specialized units of all available personnel. Luftwaffe personnel without planes and German navy (Kriegsmarine) sailors without ships were given some basic infantry training and were pressed into service. In addition, every male member of the population between the ages of 16 to 60 not previously called up for military service was forced into service in one form or another.

A final source of manpower for Hitler's last great offensive action of the war was the callback of wounded or disabled veterans. By such means, Hitler placed an additional 750,000 men under arms. He thus built up a strategic reserve consisting of 25 volksgrenadier divisions and six refitted panzer divisions with at least 150 tanks each.

To make up for the reduced numbers of men assigned to the volksgrenadier divisions, and retain the same level of firepower as found in the early war infantry divisions, they were issued with a much larger complement of automatic weapons. By the time of the Battle of the Bulge, many German volksgrenadiers and Waffen SS infantrymen were equipped with the Sturmgeweher MP-44. The MP-44 was the world's first true assault rifle. It had a 30-round box magazine and a rate of fire of 500 rounds per minute (rpm). It was a big improvement over the bolt-action rifles the German infantrymen were equipped with for most of the war.

The shortage of organic artillery support within the volksgrenadier divisions was made up with the forming of a number of nonorganic motorized artillery brigades and (werfer) rocket projector brigades. The most common rocket projector, within the late-war werfer brigades, was the 21-centimeter Nebelwerfer 42. With five launching tubes mounted on a lightweight two-wheeled trailer, the 21-centimeter Nebelwerfer 42 was a very potent weapon with a top range of 8,585 yards. The rockets fired from the 21-centimeter Nebelwerfer weighed 241.5 pounds and had a 22.4-pound high-explosive warhead.

A smaller version of the 21-centimeter Nebelwerfer 41, known as the 15-centimeter Nebelwerfer 41, had six launching tubes and was also mounted on a lightweight two-wheel trailer. It had a top range of 7,715 yards. To improve the mobility of their 15-centimeter Nebelwerfer 41 units, the Germans mounted an enlarged version, with 10 launching tubes, on the rear of a light armored half-track. This version of the 15-centimeter Nebelwerfer was referred to as the 15-centimeter Panzerwerfer 42 and had a slightly increased top range of 7,550 yards. The German rocket projectors could not compare in accuracy or range with more conventional artillery weapons. But fired in mass, they could saturate an area in a matter of seconds, and they were greatly feared by American soldiers.

---

"Indeed, I had once agreed with the observation of another senior commander who said, 'Patton can get more good work out of a mediocre bunch of staff officers than anyone I ever saw.' His principals were almost without exception holdovers from the Sicilian campaign, where their performance could be most charitably described as something less than perfect. However, five months in Europe had seasoned that staff, and the greatly matured Patton succeeded in coaxing from it the brilliant effort that characterized Third Army's turnabout in the Bulge."

Upon assuming command of the Third

Within Bastogne, McAuliffe organized the 101st Airborne Division and its supporting units into regimental task forces. Each would have its proportional share of artillery, tanks, antitank, and antiaircraft forces. Thus, the light infantry formations that constituted the bulk of the 101st Airborne Division would receive supplemental firepower in their defense duties. An American M-10 tank destroyer awaits a German attack. *National Archives*

Army shortly after his arrival in England in January 1944, Patton replaced most of the existing senior staff officers with either those who had served with him in Africa and Sicily or with cavalrymen he had known before World War II. They were totally loyal and carried out his orders quietly and efficiently.

Patton set high standards and demanded excellence, timeliness, and hard work from the entire staff. He told them:

"I've won in battle and I'm going to win again. I won because I had good commanders and staff officers. I don't fight for fun and I won't tolerate any one on my staff who doesn't…. It is inevitable for men to be killed and wounded in battle. But, there is no reason why such losses should be increased because of the incompetence and carelessness of some stupid son-of-a-bitch. I don't tolerate such men on my staff."

All of Patton's staff members knew the high standards that were expected of them, but they also worked with a sense of purpose. They worked around the clock to get a job done, but when the work was done, they relaxed. They felt no need to look occupied or to take part in "busy work," when the boss was around. On the other hand, if one of Patton's staff officers did not carry his own weight or failed to get along with the rest of the staff, he would be quickly removed.

Some German division commanders had hoped to capture Allied supplies, but none were relying on that possibility for a primary source of supply. Fuel, however, was in short supply from the beginning. Inside a Belgian farmhouse, the American crew of a 3-inch M-5 antitank gun prepares to load a round into the breech of the weapon. *National Archives*

Patton had daily meetings at 0700 hours with the chief of staff, the heads of the various headquarters sections that made up Third Army, and General Otto P. Weyland of the XIX Tactical Air Command. During these informal meetings, Patton encouraged open and frank dialogue. The resulting discussions allowed constructive criticism to be voiced and provided Patton an excellent sounding board to formulate and develop his plans.

Once Patton reached a decision and issued an order, he was firm that it not be changed. To eliminate any misunderstandings, he issued orders directly to his subordinates, but required that short, written orders reach the subordinate before they were implemented. He also suggested that army orders not exceed a page and a half of typewritten text, and that they could usually be done on one page with a sketch map on the back. These orders were to describe what to do—not how to do it.

In addition to his morning meetings, he also held more formal general staff meetings every day at 0800 hours and 1700 hours. The morning briefings were intended to keep all participants informed of current plans and operations and to make sure that all staff section planning was coordinated. Generally, these meetings lasted no longer than 20 minutes. After he was informed of the latest news, Patton would ask questions or seek advice from his staff members. Once that day's activities were outlined, Patton would leave for his tours of the Third Army's front-line positions. Upon his return, Patton would use the afternoon staff meeting to be briefed on the day's events.

Artillery units in Bastogne, like this 105-millimeter howitzer, were to play a crucial role in keeping the Germans at bay until Patton's Third Army arrived, The 105 could hurl a 33-pound shell out to maximum range of 12,500 yards. *National Archives*

Examining enemy tanks left behind in the Ardennes, after the Germans withdrew from the battlefield. The U.S. Army determined that in several battles, artillery had accounted for a large share of the German tanks knocked out. American soldiers pose in front of a destroyed German turretless tank destroyer known as the Jagdpanther. *Frank Schulz collection*

In the forward areas, Patton gained a true feel for the current situation. He required one officer from each staff section to go forward each day and visit the corresponding officers of the next lower echelon. These visits provided better information for staff actions and promoted an unequaled level of understanding and solidarity between all elements of the Third Army. The line and staff knew each other well and functioned as a team.

## American Reinforcements to the Ardennes

In addition to elements from the 7th and 10th Armored Divisions, Eisenhower ordered the 82nd and 101st Airborne Divisions to the Ardennes sector. Both divisions were at rest in France when Eisenhower ordered them into action, the 82nd Airborne toward St. Vith and the 101st to Bastogne. Because Bastogne had been the VIII Corps headquarters prior to the German offensive, headquarters personnel from the VIII Corps were leaving the area as the 101st Airborne Division arrived in Bastogne.

The 101st Airborne Division was a well-trained veteran unit consisting of 805 officers and 11,035 enlisted men. Included in its organization were four infantry regiments and various support groups. The division commander, Major General Maxwell D. Taylor, was in the United States when the German attack struck, and his second in command was in England. As third in charge, Brigadier General Anthony C. McAuliffe, the division's artillery commander, took over command of the division.

The U.S. Army's traditional doctrine for countering a large penetration like the one in the Ardennes formed the basis of Eisenhower's plan. The first step would be to hold the shoulders of the penetration to prevent the enemy from expanding the base of his salient. Then, crucial choke points, such as St. Vith and Bastogne, would be cut off to restrict the advance of the enemy forces by denying them full use of routes of advance. The final step would be to counterattack along the flanks of the penetration to cut off and destroy advancing enemy forces. To implement this course of action, Eisenhower knew he would have to completely change his three army groups (the 21st, 12th, and the 6th) from their ongoing offensive plans to a defense posture in all but the Ardennes sector.

Eisenhower ordered the 6th Army Group, on the southern flank of Patton's Third Army, to shift its forces so that it could move its boundary northward to cover a large portion of the Third Army sector. This would free the Third Army commander to launch an early counterattack into the southern flank of the German penetration in the Ardennes.

On December 18, Eisenhower distributed a message to his top subordinates stating:

"The enemy is making a major thrust and

On December 19, small German units, consisting of both infantry and tanks, both with and without artillery support, try to infiltrate through the defensive lines of the 101st Airborne Division around Bastogne under cover of bad weather. An American 81-millimeter mortar team prepares to fire its weapon. *National Archives*

still has reserves uncommitted. It appears that he will be prepared to employ the whole of his armored reserve to achieve success. My intention is to take immediate action to check the enemy advance, and then to launch a counteroffensive without delay with all forces north of the Moselle."

Eisenhower soon supplemented this message with instructions that:

"The German line of advance must not be permitted to cross the Meuse River."

Eisenhower did not want the large number

Inside Bastogne the American defenders could call on the support of over 130 artillery pieces. The crew of this American 8-inch howitzer prepares for a firing mission. It could hurl a 200-pound shell out to maximum range of 18,150 yards. *National Archives*

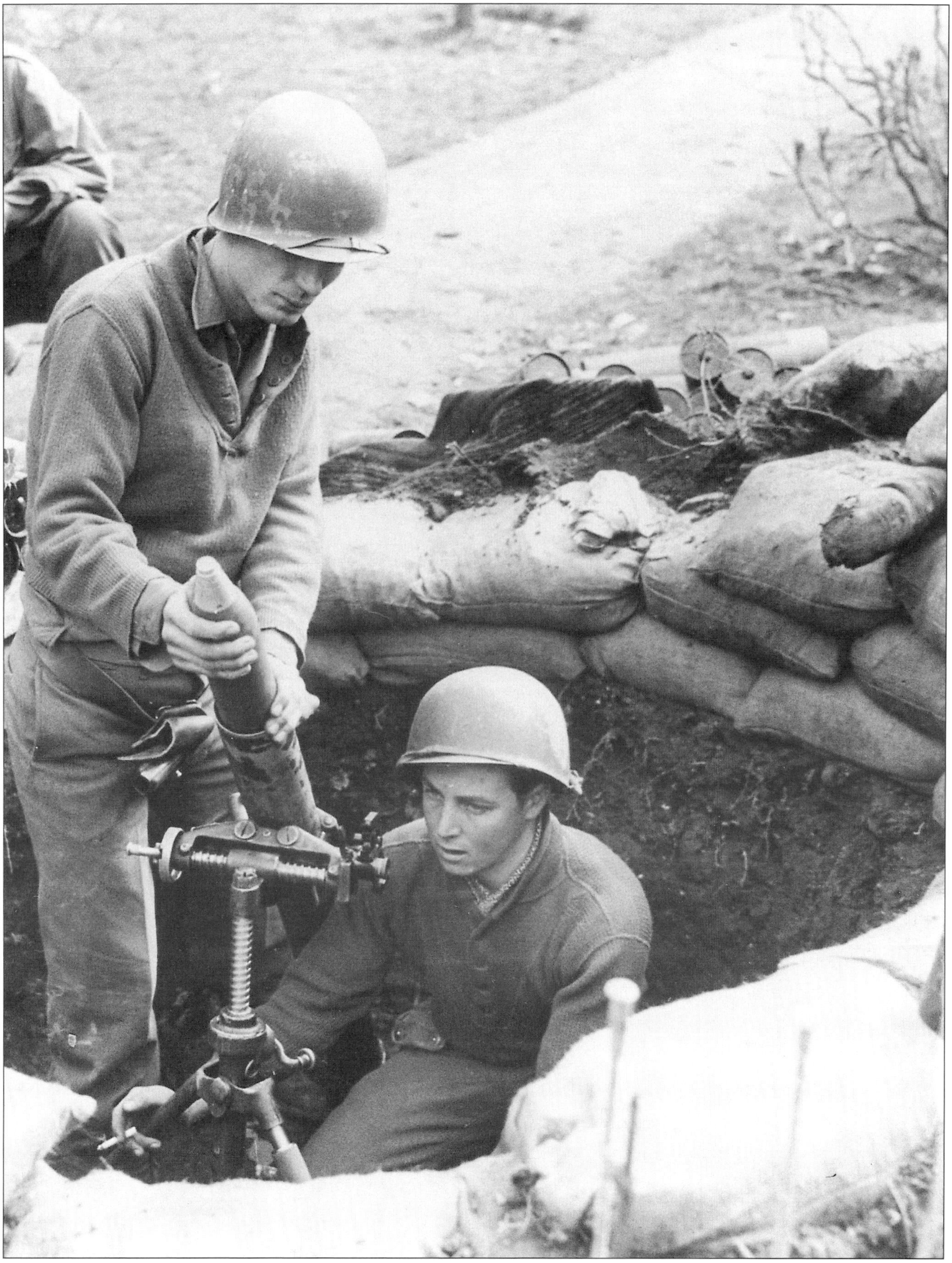

of Allied supply dumps on the western side of the Meuse to fall into enemy hands. He feared that if the German offensive operation reached these critical supplies, especially fuel, the Germans could rupture the entire Allied line.

In response to Eisenhower's message, Patton noted:

"At the direction of the army commander (Bradley) I reported to his headquarters in Luxembourg, accompanied by G-2, G-3, and G-4 of the Third Army. The situation of the enemy breakthrough, as then known, was explained.

"General Bradley asked when I could intervene. I stated I could do so with three divisions very shortly. I then telephoned Chief of Staff Third Army and directed that the attack of the 4th Armored and 80th Infantry Divisions be halted and sufficient transportation to move the 80th Division anytime after dawn of the 19th be collected, and that the Fourth Armored Division be prepared to move the night 18-19 December. Also, I directed that the XIX Tactical Air Command be notified that the blitz was off for the present.

"General Bradley called at 2200 hours and stated that the situation was worse than it had been at noon and directed that the troops as per previous paragraph be moved as rapidly as possible. Also that General Milliken move forward echelon of his headquarters to the front. I suggested Arlon. This was approved. General Bradley further ordered that General Millikin report in person to the Chief of Staff Twelfth Army Group on the morning of the 19th; and that I, accompanied by one staff officer, meet General Bradley for a conference with General Eisenhower at Verdun at 1100 the same date.

"One CC of the 4th Armored moved at midnight on Longwy, followed by remainder of divi-

In conjunction with the strong American defensive measures around Bastogne, the German attackers were hampered by the inadequate road network, and by not having enough supply trucks. These factors combined together were greatly slowing the German advance. American soldiers look out from a building they successfully defended from a German infantry attack. The closeness of the fighting can be clearly demonstrated by the dead German soldier lying at the foot of the building. *National Archives*

sion at dawn. The 80th Infantry started to move on Luxembourg at dawn December 19. The G-4 of the Twelfth Army Group facilitated these operations by a rapid collection of truck companies from Com. Z (communications zone)."

On December 19, Eisenhower summoned his senior commanders to a meeting at Verdun, France, to issue additional orders for stopping the German Ardennes counteroffensive. Before leaving for Verdun, Patton addressed his Third Army staff by stating:

"What has occurred up north is no occasion for excitement. As you know, alarm spreads very quickly in a military command. You must be extremely careful in a critical situation such as this not to give rise to any undue concern among the troops. Our plans have been changed. We're going to fight, but in a different place. Also, we are going to have to move very fast. We pride ourselves on our ability to move quickly. But, we're going to have to do it faster now than we're ever done before. I have no doubt that we will meet all demands made on us. You always have and I know you will do so again this time. And whatever happens, we will keep on doing as we have always done, killing Germans wherever we find the sons-of-bitches."

At the Verdun meeting Eisenhower calmly announced:

"The present situation is to be regarded as one of opportunity for us and not of disaster. There will be only cheerful faces at this conference table."

Patton, who had often criticized his boss for being too cautious in the past, was very pleased with Eisenhower's comments. It meant to Patton that Eisenhower had grasped the fact that this was a golden opportunity to destroy the last major reserve of German forces

On December 20 and 21, the Germans continued their small-unit infiltration methods with some limited success. Bastogne continued to be a matter of concern to XLVII Corps. It was believed on December 20 that, with advances continuing north and south of the town, Bastogne would soon be encircled and that the 26th Volksgrenadier Division following the panzer divisions could capture it without too much trouble. An American soldier armed with a Browning Automatic Rifle (BAR) takes a German soldier prisoner. *National Archives*

76   Patton and the Battle of the Bulge

Even though the Germans had encircled Bastogne on December 21, the 26th Volksgrenadier Division was not strong enough to take it. In an effort to bluff the American defenders inside Bastogne to surrender, the German commander of the XLVII Panzer Corps composed the now famous surrender note on the evening of December 21. After the note was delivered to the commander of the 101st Airborne Division in Bastogne on December 22, the German commander received his famous reply: "Nuts." Infantrymen manning a .30-caliber (water-cooled) machine gun look out from their defensive position. *National Archives*

in the west, now that they had ventured forth from behind the protection of the Siegfried Line. Not able to contain his excitement, Patton blurted out:

"Hell, let's have the guts to let the sons-of-bitches go all the way to Paris, then we'll really cut 'em off and chew 'em up! "

Bastogne was completely surrounded by the Germans on December 21. The 101st Airborne Division still maintained communication with VIII Corps headquarters, now located in the town of Arlon, Belgium, by radio. Despite the extreme vulnerability of telephone lines throughout the Battle of the Bulge, it would remain the preferred means of communication in the U.S. Army. This American soldier, however, is using a handie-talkie radio SCR 536. The radios used in late 1944 lacked the necessary range and constantly failed in the woods and hills of the Ardennes. *National Archives*

To the other senior American commanders present at the meeting, Patton's comment seemed to be out of place. Eisenhower responded:

"George, that's fine. But the enemy must never be allowed to cross the Meuse."

Eisenhower then asked Patton how long before the Third Army could launch a counterattack into the south of the German penetration. Patton joyfully announced that his army could attack "on December 22 with three divisions!" Not realizing that Patton had been preparing for this change in direction for several days, the others in the room expressed stunned disbelief.

Colonel Charles R. Codman, Patton's aide, described the reaction:

On December 22, the day the Germans delivered the note demanding Bastogne's surrender, they carried out a series of small attacks along the town's defensive perimeter. Only two attacks of any significance, neither larger than company size, occurred. Two American soldiers look over a captured German Sturmgewehr 44 (StG-44) assault rifle. The StG-44 fired a 7.92-millimeter bullet from a 30-round curved magazine. *National Archives*

"There was a stir, a shuffling of feet, as those present straightened up in their chairs. In some faces, skepticism. But through the room the current of excitement leaped like a flame. To disengage three divisions actually in combat and launch them over more than 100 miles of icy roads straight into the heart of a major attack of unprecedented violence presented problems which few commanders would have undertaken to resolve in that length of time."

Most of the senior commanders in the room considered it impossible for Patton to shift his forces 90 degrees from a major eastern offensive to one toward the north in such a short time. Eisenhower concluded from Patton's statement that he was underestimating the actual strength of the German attack. Eisenhower also believed that three divisions would not have enough combat power to successfully carry out the kind of attack he knew would be necessary to cut off the advancing German armies. After Patton explained that he would follow up his initial three-division attack with one of three more soon after, Eisenhower approved the plan."

On December 19, Eisenhower also decided to turn over temporary control of American forces north of the Ardennes (most of Hodges' First Army and all of Simpson's Ninth Army) to Montgomery and his 21st Army Group. Bradley's only remaining First Army corps, Middleton's VIII Corps, was attached to Patton's Third Army for the upcoming operation. Bradley saw the rearrangement of command by Eisenhower as a lack of confidence in his leadership abilities.

Eisenhower had high hopes that by giving Montgomery the bulk of Bradley's 12th Army Group, he would commit his reserve forces to counterattacking the northern flank of the German penetration in the Ardennes. The strategy preferred by Eisenhower would involve Montgomery and Patton counterattacking the German penetration at the same time. This would prevent the Germans from concentrating their resources on just one threat at a time. If both Montgomery's and Patton's counterattacks were successful, there was a good chance at cutting off the German advance at its base, thus trapping the bulk of enemy forces within the Ardennes. However, Montgomery delayed his first counterattack to early January 1945.

Despite the lack of help from Montgomery's forces arrayed on the northern flank of the Ardennes, Patton, with the full support of Eisenhower and Bradley, quickly set out to counterattack the southern flank of the German penetration in the Ardennes. There was little time to waste, since the XLVII Panzer Corps of Manteuffel's Fifth Panzer Army had already cut off and surrounded the American units in Bastogne.

Patton described the crucial events of December 19 in his notes:

"Meeting of all corps commanders and the commanding general of the XIX Tactical Air Command (TAC) and the general staff of the Third Army was called at 0800. The new situation was explained. I stated that the reputation

On December 23 small German attacks continued to the west and southeast of Bastogne, but the weather had cleared and American air power was beginning to take its toll of German forces and equipment. A twin-engine American-built Douglas A-26B Invader makes a bombing run over the Ardennes. Besides its bomb load, the A-26B had six Browning .50-caliber machine guns fitted in its nose for the ground attack role. *Real War Photos*

of the Third Army and XIX Tactical Air Command for speed and effectiveness resulted from the efficiency of the officers present, and that I counted upon them for even greater successes.

"On the assumption that the VII Corps would be assigned to Third Army, a plan for the employment of III and VII Corps was drawn up. Three possible lines of attack were envisaged: Neufchâteau-St. Hubert; Arlon-Bastogne; Luxembourg-Diekirch-St. Vith.

"A brief telephone code between myself and the Chief of Staff, Third Army, was drawn up.

"Left for Verdun at 0930, arriving at 1045.

"As a result of the conference, the supreme commander directed that the 6th Army Group take over the southern front as far north as the southern boundary of the XX Corps. Third Army; the 6th Armored Division to stay in the Saarbrucken area until relieved by elements of the Seventh Army. The 87th and 42nd Infantry Divisions of the Third Army to pass to the Seventh Army.

"At this moment, it seemed to me probable that the Third Army in its new role, would be constituted as follows:

"VIII Corps (General Middleton) in vicinity of Neufchâteau—101st Airborne Division, and elements of 28th Infantry, 9th and 10th Armored Divisions, and 106th Infantry Division, plus corps troops. III Corps (General Milliken) in vicinity of Arlon—26th Infantry, 80th Infantry, and Fourth Armored Divisions. The XXI Corps (General Eddy) to be assembled in vicinity of Luxembourg—consisting of 35th, 4th, and 5th Infantry Divisions and elements of the 9th and 10th Armored Divisions. The XX Corps (General Walker) in vicinity of Thionville—90th and 95th Infantry Divisions,

THE GERMAN ATTACK AND AMERICAN REACTION 79

By December 23, the German situation regarding Bastogne was becoming increasingly frustrating. Army Group B continued to insist on the town being taken in conjunction with the advance to the Meuse. To this end, the XLVII Corps commander was informed that he was to have additional divisions put under his control. An American two-man bazooka team test fires at an abandoned German Panther tank. *National Archives*

6th Armored Division when relieved by Seventh Army, and Task Force Polk.

"In reply to a question from General Eisenhower as to when the Third Army could attack to the north, I stated it could attack with III Corps on the 23rd of December.

"After meeting at Verdun, I called Chief of Staff Third Army on phone and gave following instructions: 26th Infantry Division to be moved December 20 to vicinity of Arlon, advanced detachments to move at once. The XII Corps to disengage, and corps headquarters and artillery to move to vicinity of Luxembourg 21st of December, leaving a working headquarters at old location until such time as it could be relieved by XV Corps, Seventh Army. Thirty-fifth Infantry Division to be withdrawn from line and assembled at Metz. Tactical Echelon Third Army Headquarters to move on Luxembourg 20th of December. Forward Echelon III Corps to move to the vicinity of Arlon at once."

### The Fight for Bastogne

Though surrounded, the 101st Airborne Division and the other units inside Bastogne were not cut off. They still had radio communication with Middleton's VIII Corps and knew a relief column from Patton's Third Army would soon be pushing toward them.

That Bastogne was still in American hands on December 21 was due to a number of factors.

A major factor was Manteuffel's refusal to allow Luettwitz (the XLVII Panzer Corps commander) to devote all his resources to seizing Bastogne during the opening stages of Hitler's Ardennes counteroffensive. Another problem was the inability of the Fifth Panzer Army to bring up its divisional and corps level artillery assets from the initial line of departure (east of the Our River) during the early stages of their advance. This resulted from both the lack of good east-west roads in the area as well as a shortage of engineer (pioneer) bridging units in the German Army by that time in the war.

The Fifth Panzer Army commander insisted that the 26th Volksgrenadier Division, with some minor help from the Panzer Lehr Division, could take Bastogne without additional help. Manteuffel correctly felt that reaching the Meuse was a critical goal of the Fifth Panzer Army during the early stages of the operation.

Another contributing factor that allowed the 101st to reach Bastogne shortly before Luettwitz's XLVII Corps, was the valiant performance of Conbatt Command B (CCB) of the 10th Armored Division, and Reserve Combat Command (CCR) of the 9th Armored Division. Through a series of fierce roadblock battles to the east of Bastogne over a three-day period, they managed to blunt the advance elements of the Panzer Lehr Division long enough for McAuliffe to rush his lead regiment (the 501st Airborne Infantry) in to relieve them. This resulted in the first combat action for the 101st during the Battle of the Bulge.

The paratroopers of the 101st were supported by one 105-millimeter battery from their 907th Glider Field Artillery Battalion. The Panzer Lehr Division suffered over 80 casualties from the 105-millimeter battery during the first hour of battle. The airborne gunners had set up 1,000 yards behind the paratroopers, and their howitzers could easily be heard along the battle line. The sharp crack of the 105-millimeter howitzers fooled the German divisional commander of the Panzer Lehr into thinking that more American tanks had arrived. The German commander halted his attack and withdrew his forces—a serious mistake that eventually cost the Germans the Bastogne.

The organic artillery support for the 101st Airborne consisted of one 105-millimeter and three 75-millimeter field artillery battalions. (There were three batteries of four guns each within a World War II era artillery battalion.) In addition to its own organic fire support, the 101st was aided in its defense of Bastogne by a number of other attached units. They included 40 tanks from CCB of the 10th Armored Division, 54 M-18 Hellcats (armed with a high-velocity 76-millimeter gun) from the 705th Tank Destroyer Battalion, and 2 battalions of 155-millimeter howitzers. These units and a makeshift replacement pool of stragglers (including artillery units) referred to as Team Snafu, beefed up the defensive capabilities of the 101st throughout the siege. By the evening of December 20, McAuliffe had a force under his command totaling 18,000 men and at least 130 artillery pieces.

On the evening of December 21, Luettwitz composed the now famous "ultimatum" note addressed to the defenders of Bastogne that demanded: "the honorable surrender of the encircled town" in two hours on threat of "annihilation" by the massed fire of German artillery. This was a bluff by the German commander, since the Americans inside Bastogne outnumbered him in both troops and firepower. McAuliffe, commander of all the American forces defending Bastogne, expressed his contempt for the German offer of surrender with his famous reply "Nuts," which was delivered to the Germans the next day. When the Germans proved puzzled by the term, another American officer was kind enough to explain to the Germans that it meant "Go to hell."

After the enemy surrender offer was rejected, the Germans launched more probing attacks along the entire Bastogne defensive perimeter. All were repulsed. On December 23 the enemy probes continued, but the weather had cleared and American air power was beginning to take its toll on the German forces surrounding Bastogne. An aerial resupply system had also been put into effect that same day, bringing badly needed supplies to the 101st Airborne Division, sending American morale soaring.

The Germans, on the other hand, were becoming increasingly upset about the situation at Bastogne. Manteuffel's Fifth Panzer Army was now on the defensive almost everywhere, and the possibility of advancing to the Meuse and Antwerp had by now evaporated. Luettwitz was informed on December 23 that the 9th Panzer Division and 15th Panzergrenadier (armored infantry) Division would come under his corps control on December 24. Luettwitz was also told that the 3d Panzergrenadier Division was on its way to assist in the capture of Bastogne. Despite these strong reinforcements, the numerous attacks launched by Luettwitz's Corps on Bastogne on December 24 and 25 were uncoordinated, and all failed.

On the evening of December 25, Luettwitz became highly concerned about the probability of a relief column from Patton's Third Army breaking through to Bastogne. He asked Manteuffel's Fifth Panzer headquarters staff for either additional reinforcements or permission to call off his attacks on Bastogne. Luettwitz's request for assistance was denied, as was his request for permission to withdraw.

Chapter Three

# The Road to Bastogne

Eisenhower was informed by his intelligence chief on December 20 that Hitler had committed everything he had to the Ardennes counteroffensive. With no uncommitted German reserves, the Allies could counterattack in the Ardennes sector with little risk. Since poor weather conditions had grounded Allied and German reconnaissance planes, the Allies were able to regroup for a surprise counterattack along both flanks of the German penetration.

A top-level meeting called by Eisenhower on December 19 at Verdun, France, was in response to the German counteroffensive in the Ardennes. It was attended by all of Eisenhower's top generals, and it set in motion a series of actions that would quickly regain the initiative lost by the Allies during the early stages of their Ardennes counteroffensive. The 13 American commanders on the western front assembled on October 10, 1944. In the front row, left to right, stand Patton, Bradley, Eisenhower, Hodges, and Simpson. *National Archives*

The counterattacks were to begin when Patton's Third Army in the south and Montgomery's 21st Army Group in the north were strong enough to attack.

The immediate goal of the planned counterattack against the south flank of the German penetration was to reach Bastogne. Once contact was made with the American defenders, Patton's troops were tasked with the job of restoring and maintaining a permanent corridor into the town. They were also instructed to push the German units surrounding Bastogne away from the town's road network so it could be used by the Third Army as a base for further operations to the north and northeast.

Patton chose the newly arrived III Corps (under the command of Major General John Millikin) to lead the advance toward Bastogne. The III Corps attack was to begin on December 22, from an assembly area in Belgium near the town of Arlon, only 20 miles south of Bastogne. Bastogne could be reached by the Arlon-Bastogne road on the right, or the Neufchâteau-Bastogne road about 20 miles east of Arlon. Millikin and his III Corps staff preferred the Arlon route, where the Fourth Armored Division was already positioned to attack. Major General Troy H. Middleton, the VIII Corps commander, favored a broad thrust using both routes with the main thrust along the Neufchâteau-Bastogne road. After some discussion, the Arlon-Bastogne road was chosen for its direct line to Bastogne. If the Arlon approach could be seized, it would also stop the reinforcement of the German troops already south of Bastogne (the

5th Parachute Division and the 325th Volksgrenadier Division).

Patton wrote in his notes on December 20:

"I visited 12th Army Group at Luxembourg, then the commanding generals of the III and VIII Corps and Fourth Armored Division at Arlon. Later visited Headquarters 4th and 26th Infantry Divisions, 9th and 10th Armored Divisions, and the Advanced Echelon 80th Division, which had just reached Luxembourg.

"As it was apparent that for the present the VIII Corps had no offensive power, it was directed to hold Bastogne with the 101st Airborne Division and following attachments: one CC of the 9th Armored and one CC of the 10th Armored Divisions; the 705th TD Bn (battalion), less one company; and some corps artillery. Remainder of the corps to fall back, using delaying action and demolitions.

"The III Corps is to attack with the purpose of relieving Bastogne on 22nd of December at 0600. The commanding general 10th Armored Division was directed to take temporary command of XII Corps pending arrival of that headquarters. Also to incorporate in his unit one CC of the 9th Armored Division in the vicinity of Luxembourg. The commanding general of the 9th Armored Division with his headquarters was sent to VIII Corps to take over command of two combat commands of the 9th Armored and one combat command of the 10th Armored Division.

"Through the chief of staff Third Army, arranged for immediate movement to new theater of combat of all self-propelled tank destroyer battalions and separate tank battalions, necessary ammunition, engineers, and hospitals.

"Also, that the 5th Division be disengaged at Saarlautern and be moved on to Luxembourg at once."

The sector chosen for the III Corps advance lay within the eastern part of Luxembourg and the western part of Belgium. It contained some of the most rugged terrain in all of the

A few very scary days had to pass before the first American counterattacks could be launched in the Ardennes, and the Americans could wrest the initiative back from the German attackers. To gain time and save lives, Eisenhower was willing to let his forces fall back as far as the Meuse River, but no farther. The gun crew of a towed 3-inch antitank gun clean the barrel of its weapon. *National Archives*

Ardennes. The large Sure and Wiltz Rivers ran through the area and represented tough obstacles for the advance of any mechanized or motorized formations from the south. Numerous other smaller rivers and streams of varying width and depth also crisscrossed the entire region.

The forces assigned to the III Corps consisted of the 26th and 80th Infantry Divisions as well as the elite Fourth Armored Division. Millikin's orders called for him to advance north with his three divisions in a line-abreast formation. The 80th Infantry Division would be on the right, and would maintain contact during its advance with the left wing of Patton's XII Corps. The 26th Division would form the center. The Fourth Armored Division would advance on the left with Bastogne as its goal.

From the first moment of planning on the advance of III Corps to Bastogne, there was no doubt in that Patton's main focus would be the progress of the Fourth Armored Division. Patton had promised Bradley that he would be inside the town by Christmas Day. The 26th

Eisenhower was well aware of Patton's desire to attack at once with whatever forces were available to him. This was not the manner in which the more cautious Eisenhower liked to conduct military operations. On the other hand, Eisenhower, here with Patton in the Ardennes, recognized that the continued occupation of Bastogne, the key to the entire road net on the south side of the German penetration in the Ardennes, was essential to future offensive operations. Eisenhower therefore decided to allow Patton to make a narrow thrust aimed at relieving Bastogne. *National Archives*

and 80th Infantry Divisions were primarily seen as providing a flank guard to the advance of the Fourth Armored Division.

The Fourth Armored Division had arrived in France slightly more than a month after the Normandy landings of June 6, 1944, as a part of Patton's Third Army. It was soon in the thick of the action, leading the American army breakout from the Normandy beachhead (Operation Cobra). In the month-long pursuit of the defeated German forces across central France that followed, the division was always in the vanguard of the Third Army. By the time the division crossed the Meuse on August 21, 1944, it had traveled over 700 miles.

The division sped off in the direction of the Ardennes under Major General Hugh J. Gaffey, Patton's former chief of staff. Before taking command of the Fourth Armored Division, Gaffey had never commanded a full division in combat, so Patton prescribed the tactics to be used by Gaffey and the 4th Armored:

"The attack should lead off with the tanks, artillery, tank destroyers, and armored engineers in the van. The main body of armored infantry should be kept back. If stiff resistance is encountered, envelopment tactics should be used. No close-in envelopment should be attempted; all envelopments should be started a mile or a mile and a half mile back, and be made at right angles."

A colorful description of the deployment of the Fourth Armored Division for the attack on Bastogne comes from the division's official history. It begins:

"Bastogne was at the end of a 130-mile 'fire call' run the Fourth Armored made to smash back the German winter offensive in the Ardennes. The run started at Fenetrange, where the division was resting in the French Lorraine from exhausting battles against mud, cold, and German armor east of the Sarre.

Eisenhower and Bradley share a moment of humor. Even as Eisenhower gave Patton permission to launch an attack toward Bastogne, he made it clear to Bradley that he had to restrain his subordinate from undertaking any more ambitious plans. Patton's advance to Bastogne would be in Eisenhower's words: "only be a steppingstone for the main counteroffensive." *National Archives*

Divisions assigned to the III Corps for its attack on the German penetration in the Ardennes consisted of the 26th Infantry Division, the 80th Infantry Division, and the Fourth Armored Division. All had been out of the line or in a quiet sector when the Third Army was ordered north. This American crew has its Browning .50-caliber (water-cooled) machine gun set up in the Ardennes as an antiaircraft weapon. *National Archives*

"On December 18, the division was in XII Corps reserve. Tankers heard vague reports of a two-day old German offensive up in Belgium and Luxembourg, but gave it little thought. But at 1700, orders were received to march north against the breakthrough. CCB was to move at midnight. At 2300, CCB was ready. Shortly before midnight, the combat command got its march route from army.

"Trucks, weapons carriers, tanks, half-tracks, armored cars, and peeps (jeeps) jammed the roads, and somehow kept moving northeast. Through overcast days and blackout at night, Third Army's divisions rolled to the western front's bloodiest battleground. Drivers strained bloodshot eyes at cat's eye blackout lights on vehicles ahead. Infantrymen slept with M-1s between their knees. When they had to relieve themselves they urinated over the tailgates of the jolting six-by-sixes. In the incredibly short period of two days, Third Army was on the south flank of the 40-mile German penetration. The march, an average of 120-

Before Patton's III Corps began its counterattack, it was known that the German units had already moved beyond Bastogne. It was presumed that the Arlon-Bastogne road had been cut, but even this was not certain. A wounded American soldier, his face blocked out by a wartime censor, rides on the hood of a litter jeep. *National Archives*

THE ROAD TO BASTOGNE 85

Elements of four German divisions were supposed to be in the line opposite Patton's III Corps: the 5th Parachute Division and the 212th, 276th, and 352d Volksgrenadier Divisions. All but the 5th Parachute Division had been identified days earlier as belonging to the German Seventh Army. Curious American soldiers are inspecting a destroyed German StuG III (turretless tank destroyer). *National Archives*

What the German divisions facing Patton's III Corps would do in response to an American attack was anybody's guess. The III Corps attack would have to push off through a thin screen of friendly troops whose positions were uncertain, against an enemy whose exact location was unknown, over terrain that had not been scouted. The American crew of an M-5 light tank white-washes its vehicle to blend in with the surroundings. *Patton Museum*

The Germans were equally in the dark as to the III Corps capabilities and intentions. The 26th Infantry Division could not be located by German intelligence after it left Metz, France, and would not be identified as present in its new sector until two days after the American advance began. A long, fog-shrouded infantry column is on the march in the Ardennes. *Real War Photos*

miles for Fourth Armored troops, was the longest made by any division as Third Army wheeled its front about 90 degrees with speed that appalled the Germans."

## The Fourth Armored Division's Advance to Bastogne

Gaffey, under Patton's direction, sent Combat Commands A and B of the Fourth Armored Division into the attack in a line-abreast formation. The advance was scheduled to begin in the early morning hours of December 22. CCA would advance along the main Arlon-Bastogne road, while CCB pushed forward on secondary roads to the west. Information available to Gaffey and Patton indicated that the bridges across the Sure River, at the town of Martelange, had been destroyed. In the event that CCA was delayed at the Sure River crossings,

THE ROAD TO BASTOGNE 87

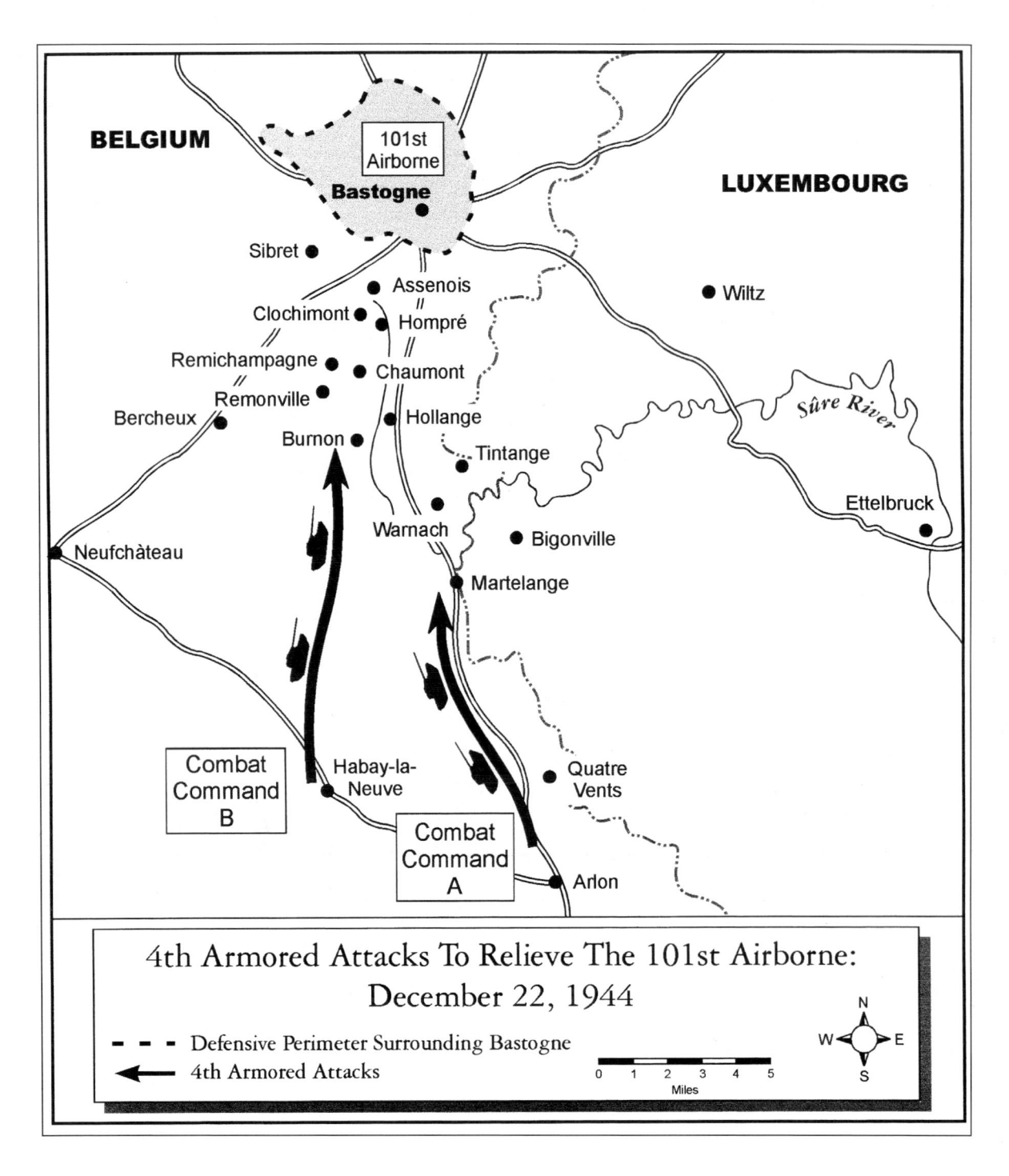

### 4th Armored Attacks To Relieve The 101st Airborne: December 22, 1944

CCB was to move eastward and take the lead ahead of CCA on the main Arlon-Bastogne road. In either case, CCB, under the command of Brigadier General Holmes Dager, was designated to lead the Fourth Armored Division into Bastogne.

On December 22, as CCB advanced along the snow-covered Arlon-Bastogne road, it ran into its first delay near the town of Martelange, 12 miles south of Bastogne, where it had to bridge a large crater. CCB also entered into a firefight with elements of the 5th Parachute Division, and it was morning before the German resistance was overcome. CCA finally crossed the Sure on the afternoon of December 23, with the objective of reaching Bastogne that night.

Meanwhile, CCB, advancing on the west of CCA along a series of secondary roads, was also making good progress. By noon,

Patton inspected the three divisions of the III Corps on December 20 and concluded that they were ready for action. The corps would advance north in the general direction of St. Vith, located 10 miles northeast of Bastogne. On alert in the Ardennes, an American gun crew waits with its 40-millimeter antiaircraft gun. It could fire up to 120 rounds (weighing 1.96 pounds each) per minute up to a maximum ceiling of 23,622 feet. *National Archives*

CCB was close to the small village of Buron, only 7 miles from Bastogne. The Germans seemed to offer very little opposition to the advance of CCB. Encouraged by this lack of enemy resistance, Patton ordered that CCB continue its advance through the night to reach Bastogne. The village of Buron was cleared by elements of CCB by midnight. As the advance guard of CCB carefully made its way through the darkness toward Chaumont, the next village on the road to Bastogne, it encountered only occasional small arms fire. On reaching the outskirts of Chaumont, however, the level of German resistance increased, forcing the advance guard of CCB to withdraw.

The next morning, the full force of CCB was brought to bear on the 26th Volksgrenadier Division, the German defenders of Chaumont. American fighter-bombers from the XIX TAC also attacked the village in support of their comrades on the ground. Despite repeated attacks by the main force of CCB, the Germans would not give up. At one point in the battle for Chaumont, the Germans counterattacked with a force of 15 self-propelled tank destroyers. Caught by surprise, CCB was thrown back with the loss of 11 tanks and 65 men. Chaumont would not fall into American hands until December 23. By the time the battle was over, CCB had inflicted heavy losses on the 5th Parachute Division. On the other hand, CCB was no closer to Bastogne and had only 10 medium tanks remaining.

In the U.S. Army in World War II, the standard heavy artillery piece, found at divisional level, was the 155-millimeter gun. It could fire a 92.6-pound shell out to a maximum range of 25,395 yards. This 155-millimeter gun has just been unhitched from its towing tractor, in the background, and is being prepared for a firing mission. *National Archives*

As CCB first reached Chaumont, CCA was finally moving over a repaired bridge at the town of Martelange. Knowing it would take time for all the elements of CCA to push across the narrow bridge, CCA rushed a small task

THE ROAD TO BASTOGNE 89

Assistance for the infantry divisions of Patton's III Corps was provided by the attachment of tank and tank destroyer battalions. Two American M-10 tank destroyers fire their 3-inch guns in the darkness. *National Archives*

By November 1944, many American tank destroyer units had begun receiving the new M-36 tank destroyer armed with a modified 90-millimeter antiaircraft gun. Like its predecessor, the M-10, the M-36 was based on the lightly armored chassis of the M-4 Sherman tank series. *Bob Fleming*

force forward in an attempt to reach Bastogne as quickly as possible. Pushing aside scattered German resistance, the CCA task force made good progress until it reached the small village of Warnach early in the evening of the 22nd. The German 5th Parachute Division and a battery of self-propelled tank destroyers quickly knocked out the two leading American halftracks. Since the village could not be bypassed at night, the American task force commander ordered five light tanks and 40 armored infantrymen to take the village. This attempt failed, as did a second and larger attack launched at midnight. The next morning the Americans renewed their attacks on Warnach. After a series of fierce house-to-house struggles, the German defender finally surrendered to the task force from CCA at about noon on the 24th. The Germans lost 135 men, and an equal number were taken prisoner. The American casualties numbered 68.

The CCs of the Fourth Armored Division suffered countless delays in trying to reach Bastogne. The men of the 101st Airborne Division and other units trapped inside Bastogne fought and waited for relief. Radio messages sent from Bastogne gave some not so subtle hints to the Fourth Armored Division that they could move a little faster. On the night of the 23rd McAuliffe sent the message: "Sorry I did

90    PATTON AND THE BATTLE OF THE BULGE

A large part of the effectiveness of American artillery in World War II was due to the use of small observation aircraft in the spotting role. The U.S. Army had first tested the concept of using modified civilian aircraft in the role in 1941. The success of those initial tests convinced the Army to field a number of small aircraft specially modified for that purpose. An example of that development, this Piper L-4 Grasshopper, is caught in a winter snowstorm. *National Archives*

not get to shake hands today. I was disappointed." Another message from inside Bastogne, addressed to the Fourth Armored Division on December 23 hinted: "There is only one more shopping day before Christmas."

Patton was not pleased by the progress of CCA and CCB toward Bastogne. He called III Corps headquarters and said: "There is too much piddling around. Bypass these towns and clear them up later. Tanks can operate on this ground now." Even as Patton complained to the III Corps headquarters about the various delays at Chaumont and Warnach, a third delay developed at Bigonville, a village 2 1/2 miles east of the Bastogne highway and close to the boundary between the Fourth Armored Division and the 26th Infantry Division. The gap between these two divisions suddenly became a matter of serious concern when on the night of December 22 there were reports that a large formation of German armor was moving into the area. To protect CCA's open right flank, Gaffey ordered Colonel Wendell Blanchard to form the division's Reserve Combat Command (CCR) into a balanced task force (using the 53d Armored Infantry Battalion and 37th Tank Battalion) and move quickly toward Bigonville.

On December 22, Patton's prayer for clear weather was issued on a small card to the officers and men of the Third Army. The card read:

"Almighty and most merciful Father, we humbly beseech Thee, of Thy great goodness, to restrain these immoderate rains with which we have had to contend. Grant us fair weather for Battle. Graciously hearken to us soldiers who called upon Thee that armed with Thy power, we may advance from victory to victory, and crush the oppression and wickedness of our enemies, and establish Thy justice among men and nations. Amen."

The reverse side of the card had a Christmas greeting from Patton to his men:

"To each officer in the Third United States Army, I wish a Merry Christmas. I have full confidence in your courage, devotion to duty, and skill in battle. We march in our might to complete victory. May God's blessing rest upon each of you on this Christmas Day."

Patton's prayer was answered. Beginning on December 23, there was a five-day break in the weather over the Ardennes. This allowed American air power to weaken the German forces surrounding the town and eased the later entrance of the Fourth Armored Division

Due to Allied air superiority in Europe, German artillery units were unable to employ their own small observation aircraft to spot for targets. This fact in combination with shortages of ammunition and equipment, and high casualty levels among artillery-trained specialists put German artillery units at a disadvantage during the Battle of the Bulge. This captured example of a German 149.1-millimeter gun could fire a 94.8-pound shell out to a maximum range of 26,800 yards. *Aberdeen Proving Ground Museum*

THE ROAD TO BASTOGNE 91

## TASK FORCE EZELL

Few students of World War II are aware that a task force from CCB of the Fourth Armored Division had, for a very short time, been inside of Bastogne six days prior to the dramatic breakthrough into the town on December 26, 1944 by CCR, of the 4th Armored.

The chain of events that led to the short visit to Bastogne by Task Force Ezell (named after its commander Captain Bert Ezell) began when CCB arrived in the general area of the town late on the night of December 18. At that point in time, the III Corps headquarters had not yet arrived on the scene, so Brigadier General Holmes E. Dager reported to the headquarters of Major General Troy Middleton's hard-pressed VIII Corps. Middleton's corps had not yet been transferred to Patton's Third Army, and remained under Hodges' First Army control until noon of December 19. Middleton radioed Hodges early on the morning of December 19, asking if he would employ CCB in defensive duties. Hodges told him to ask Bradley for permission to use CCB. Bradley radioed Middleton, without informing Patton or Major General Hugh J. Gaffey (the Fourth Armored Division commander), that he could employ CCB but only if necessary to hold his positions.

Middleton, who was desperately trying to stem the German attack into the Ardennes, quickly ordered the commander of CCB, Brigadier General Holmes E. Dager, to move his entire command into Bastogne to strengthen its defenses. Dager strongly protested to Middleton that this decision should not be made until the Fourth Armored Division commander, and the rest of the unit arrived in the area. After much discussion between the VIII Corps commander and CCB commander, it was eventually decided that only a task force, consisting of one company of tanks, armored infantry, and self-propelled artillery, would be sent to Bastogne in the early morning hours of December 20.

Task Force Ezell quickly reached its objective via the Neufchâteau-Bastogne road, detecting no enemy presence along its path. Once inside of Bastogne, Captain Ezell received orders from III Corps headquarters to return to CCB at 1400. What had happened is that Patton, now aware of Bradley's decision to let Middleton use CCB, had arrived in Arlon, where the rest of the Fourth Armored Division was now deployed) on the morning of December 20. During a short meeting that morning, Patton, Gaffey, and the III Corps commander made the decision that CCB, including Task Force Ezell, had to be kept together at all costs. For it was decided that CCB, along with the rest of the Fourth Armored Division would be leading the main attack toward Bastogne in another two days' time.

After receiving orders from III Corps to leave Bastogne at once, Ezell, without telling anybody within the town, told his men to turn their vehicles around and drive back the way they came in. Despite the large numbers of German armored units from the Fifth Panzer Army now passing south of Bastogne, on the way to the Meuse River, Task Force Ezell returned to its starting point uneventfully. On their return route, the task force retrieved a large number of abandoned American vehicles, some with their engines still running.

Since the end of World War II, many historians and writers have argued about the missed opportunities presented by Task Force Ezell and its uncontested arrival in Bastogne. Some have suggested that Gaffey should have exploited the moment by pushing the rest of the Fourth Armored Division into Bastogne, or used it to defend the Neufchâteau-Bastogne road, thereby keeping a route open into town. Others have suggested that the decision to withdraw Task Force Ezell from Bastogne saved it from possible destruction.

---

into Bastogne. (In actual fact, Patton's prayer card was written on December 11 and was intended to be issued just before the Third Army offensive on the Siegfried Line planned for December 19.)

After the war Manteuffel, commander of the Fifth Panzer Army, described to his Allied captors the effectiveness of Allied air power during the Battle of the Bulge:

"The activity of the enemy air force was decisive. It controlled the supply route, railways, and roads completely. In the same way, the air superiority too had a bad immediate effect on our fighting forces. When the fair weather set in, all troop movements, positioning, and other movements on the battlefield had to put up with all the difficulties caused by the almost complete lack of our air force and the superiority of the enemy air force."

Patton told his III Corps commanders that he favored an attack in column of regiments, "or in any case, lots of depth." He also told them to "drive like hell." As usual, Patton was optimistic about the upcoming operation. He felt certain that the Germans were unaware of the storm about to break over their heads. In the grip of winter, a column of American M-4 Sherman medium tanks is on the move. The lead vehicle is equipped with a 76-millimeter high-velocity gun. *National Archives*

Early on December 23, CCR of the Fourth Armored Division left Quatre-Vents, followed the main road to Martelange, then turned right onto a secondary road which angled northeast. This road was covered with ice and a great deal of time was spent moving the column slowly forward.

At about noon, the advance guard of CCR came under fire from a small wooded area near a crossroads where the unit would turn north to reach Bigonville. Due to strong enemy resistance, CCR could not make any progress toward its main objective for the rest of the day. Only after the Germans (from the 5th Parachute Division) withdrew from the wooded area near the crossroads that night, could CCR continue its advance to Bigonville. The next morning, CCR launched its attack on the town and cleared it before noon, taking over 400 German prisoners.

On December 23 a German newspaper reported:

On December 21, the Fourth Armored Division, then assembled in the French province of Lorraine, learned what its mission would be when the III Corps attack began on December 22. It was to advance north and relieve Bastogne. Vehicles like this American M-4 Sherman medium tank fitted with a bulldozer blade were designated as engineer armored vehicles and used to clear roadways or fill craters. *National Archives*

THE ROAD TO BASTOGNE  93

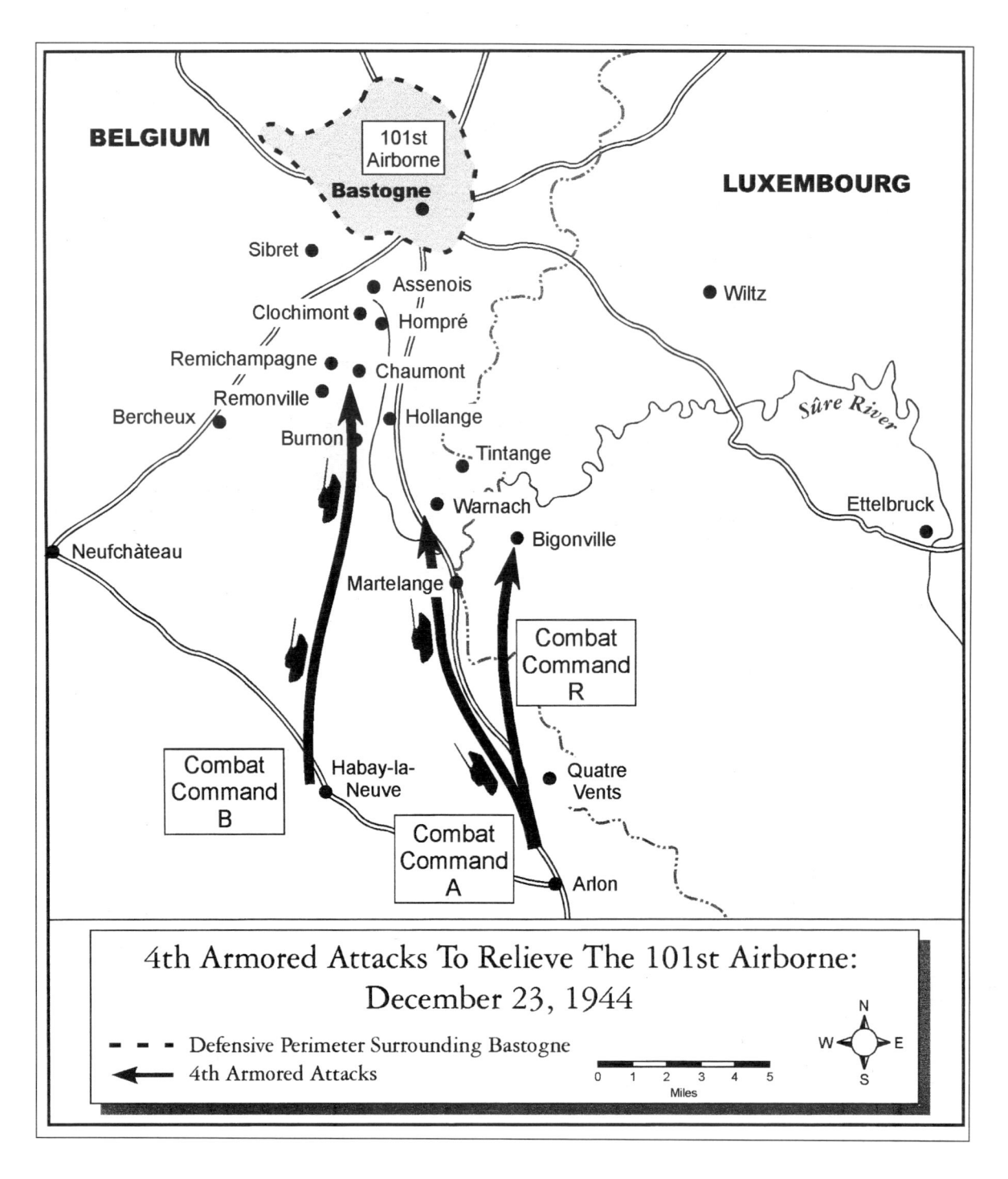

**4th Armored Attacks To Relieve The 101st Airborne: December 23, 1944**

- - - Defensive Perimeter Surrounding Bastogne
⬅ 4th Armored Attacks

"The word 'retreat' shows up everywhere in the English and American front-page-news. The Belgian population, without any shedding of tears, hauled down the flags of England and the United States, the Union Jack and the Star Spangled Banner, and stared in grim silence after the departing North Americans.

"Their 'victory' has now again withdrawn to a considerable distance, and the Germans have gained time in which to perfect their new weapons. Regarded as a whole, therefore, the war situation has changed in recent days definitely to the disadvantage of the Allies. The American troops who are surrounded in the various separate areas are fighting (Bastogne), it is true, with courage and endurance, but their enemy has captured their supply depots and cut their lines communications.

"In London, the morale barometer has reached a new low. The government is attempt-

Often found attached to American armored divisions in Europe was the 155-millimeter M-12 self-propelled gun. Based on the chassis of an obsolete M-3 medium tank, the M-12 was often the only heavy artillery available to the rapidly moving armored divisions of Patton's Third Army. *National Archives*

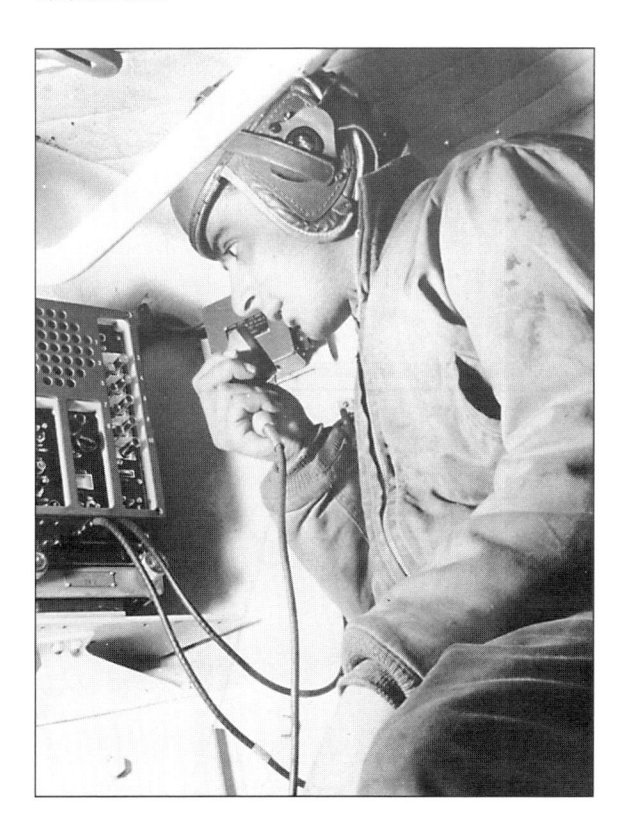

ing to cheer the public with the assurance that 'Eisenhower will find a way to handle the situation: we must just have patience.' But that is slim comfort to the sorely tried Londoners, with flying bombs hurtling through their skies, and who, in September, had been fed with the hopes that the war would be as good as ended by Christmas. The friends of Montgomery are again causing talk by asserting that the breakthrough would have been avoided if he had been in Eisenhower's place."

## New Tactics Are Needed

By Christmas Eve it was clear to both Gaffey and Millikin that leading the advance toward Bastogne with tanks was getting them

Inside an American M-10 tank destroyer, a member of the crew talks on the vehicle's onboard radio. Unlike German armored vehicles that used short-range AM radios, American armored vehicles used much more effective FM radios. *National Archives*

THE ROAD TO BASTOGNE 95

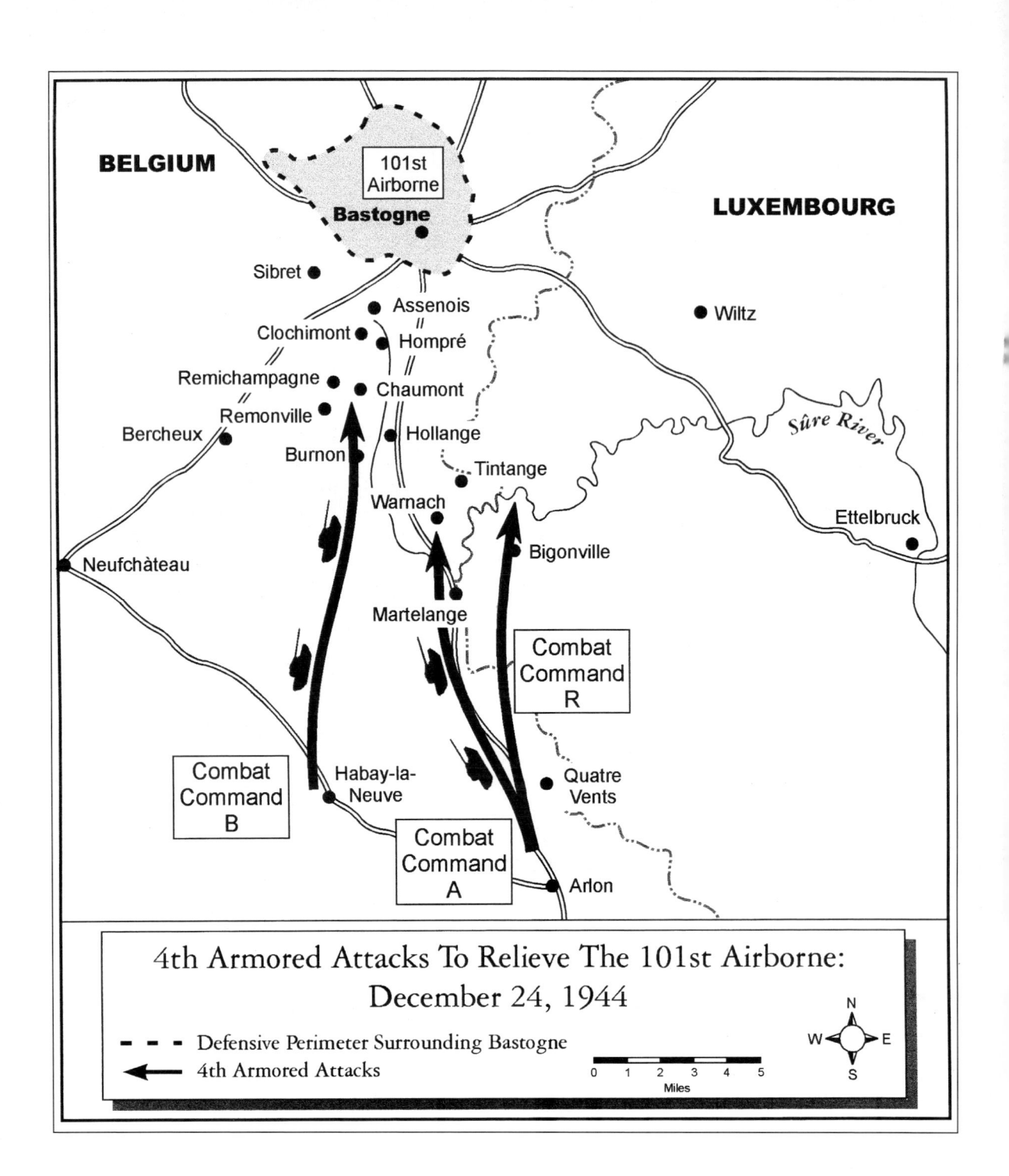


4th Armored Attacks To Relieve The 101st Airborne:
December 24, 1944

nowhere. The ice and snow-covered terrain of the Ardennes forced the American tanks to stay on the narrow hard-surfaced roads where they made easy targets for a variety of German antitank weapons. More infantry was brought forward to clear the way for the tanks of the Fourth Armored Division on the path to Bastogne, slowing the advance even further. Gaffey and Millikin also agreed that the around-the-clock tank attacks ordered by Patton and the night attacks by the infantry divisions of the III Corps had failed to achieve any significant gains. Millikin therefore ordered that all three of his divisions hold in position during Christmas Eve night, in preparation for attack early on Christmas morning.

Because all the bridges along the Arlon-Bastogne road beyond Martelange had been destroyed, Gaffey saw little chance for the tanks and armored infantry of CCR to reach Bastogne along this path. He therefore had Millikin shift the responsibility for the Bigonville sector to the 26th Infantry Division late on Christmas Eve. This freed up CCR for employment on the west flank of the III Corps, along the more easily traversed Neufchâteau-Bastogne road. To reach their new assembly area near the village of Remoiville, CCR and its 400 vehicles had to travel in a 16-mile-long column almost 30 miles at night with the moon providing the only light. During the relocation of CCR to the western flank of the Fourth Armored Division, it passed behind both CCA and CCB.

On Christmas Day, Patton wrote in his notes:

"Clear and cold. All the air up. Visited all front line divisions. Where men were in contact and could not get hot Xmas dinner, they were served chicken sandwiches.

"Exchanged the 6th Armored Division (XX Corps) with 10th Armored Division (XII Corps) effective tonight.

"The 35th Infantry Division, which closed at Metz (France) on midnight the 23rd of December, absorbed 2,000 replacements from the second 5 percent cut in corps and army troops of Third Army, all with less than a week's training. They will close north of Arlon at 1400 tomorrow, prepared to attack between the 26th Infantry and Fourth Armored Divisions the morning of the 27th. The 80th Infantry Division passes to XII Corps at 1800, the 26th."

As the Fourth Armored Division prepared itself for the Christmas Day advance toward Bastogne, Gaffey's plans still called for CCB in the center to reach Bastogne first. Both CCA and CCR were to act as flank guards during the upcoming attack. To beef up the infantry complement of the Fourth Armored Division, the 1st and 2d Infantry Battalions of the 318th Infantry were transferred in from the 80th Infantry Division. The 1st Infantry Battalion went to CCA; the 2nd Infantry Battalion went to CCB.

The 80th and 26th Infantry Divisions were located to the east of the Fourth Armored Division. The main mission of the 80th and 26th was to root out the German forces south of the Sure River and close in the north along the Sauer. This mission was important to block any efforts by the German Seventh Army to move its reserve units into the Bastogne area.

Ahead of the 80th, the German Seventh Army was already moving reinforcements into the Bastogne area on the morning of December 24. Reinforcements included the Fuehrer Grenadier Brigade and the 79th Volksgrenadier Division. Prior to this, the LXXXV Corps of the German Seventh Army had faced Millikin's III Corps with only two units, the 5th Parachute Division and the 352nd Volksgrenadier Division. Despite fears that the two German divisions in front of the American advance from the south might not hold for long, Hitler and his senior staff were very reluctant to assign Seventh Army reinforcements until it was almost too late. It was only when the threat to the German southern flank dramatically increased, as Millikin's III Corps closed in on Bastogne that reinforcements were sent to the Seventh Army.

The Fuehrer Escort Brigade was originally ordered to provide much-needed backup support for the 5th Parachute Division south of Bastogne. In this crisis, elements of the division plugged the growing gap between the 5th Parachute Division and the nearby 352nd Volksgrenadier Division. The bulk of the division was sent to prevent the American 80th

The various models of the M-4 Sherman medium tanks employed by the Fourth Armored Division had reasonably good mobility and a favorable power-to-weight ratio. They were especially prized for their mechanical reliability. This M-4 Sherman, pictured at right and below, took a hit in its hull from a high-velocity German antitank gun. *Patton Museum*

Infantry Division from crossing the Sure River east of Bastogne.

Patton was also intent on reinforcing the three-division advance of his III Corps. Patton quickly pushed the 35th Infantry Division, under the command of Major General Paul W. Baade, into the fray. On December 26, as the division came on line with the III Corps, the 80th Infantry Division was transferred from the III Corps to the XII Corps without moving from its position. Patton was reluctant to assign the XII Corps the mission of attacking northward across the cold and swollen Sure and Sauer Rivers. At almost the same time, Brandenberger, the German Seventh Army commander, was considering plans to launch a spoiling attack against the eastern flank of the American forces congregated around Bastogne. Fortunately for the American III Corps, Brandenberger was unable to muster the men or equipment to implement his plan.

### The Last Few Miles to Bastogne

On Christmas Day, 1944, all three CCs of the Fourth Armored Division were slowly grinding their way from the south toward Bastogne. That same morning, the German Fifth Panzer Army launched a strong attack against the northwest sector of the 101st's defensive perimeter around Bastogne. After some hard fighting, the German attackers were defeated.

During the heavy fighting at Warnach on December 23, a few tanks from CCA had tried to drive on to Tintange, the next village on the road to Bastogne, but had quickly bogged down. Gaffey provided reinforcements from the 80th Infantry Division to take Tintange on the way to Bastogne. After a freezing night in the snow, Major George W. Connaughton's 1st

Somewhere in the Ardennes, an American M-4 Sherman medium tank, armed with a 76-millimeter high-velocity gun, passes a destroyed German Panther medium tank. The 76-millimeter gun, as mounted on various models of the Sherman tank, was a big disappointment to American tankers, since it proved unable to punch holes in German Panther or Tiger tanks. *National Archives*

Battalion, 318th Infantry, marched off to the small creek south of the village that was their planned line of departure.

They soon discovered that the "creek" was in fact a very deep gorge. To make matters even worse, the German infantrymen on the other side of the creek were intent on defending it. Somehow, the American infantrymen succeeded in scrambling down one side of the gorge, across the creek, and up the other side under hand grenade attack. Once across the gorge, they were exposed to continuous rifle fire. Rifle fire could not stop the American advance so the Germans rolled out their single large-caliber self-propelled gun. After suffering heavy casualties from the large German assault gun, the remaining American soldiers charged the town, rather than provide ready targets for the Germans. Supported at the last minute by a formation of eight American fighter-bombers that blasted the village with bombs and rockets, the American infantrymen managed to capture Tintange, the assault gun, and the 161 German soldiers who were defending the village.

While this was going on, the 318th Infantry and the 51st Armored Infantry Battalion of CCA were capturing the village of Hollange. The village was located on the west side of the Arlon-Bastogne highway, and was only 7 miles south of Bastogne. However, the

The Fourth Armored Division had three field artillery battalions, each possessing three firing batteries equipped with the M-7 self-propelled 105-millimeter howitzer. The loader on an M-7 prepares to load a shell into the breech of the vehicle's 105-millimeter howitzer. *National Archives*

German resistance grew stronger and stronger as CCA got closer to Bastogne.

The 2nd Battalion, 318th Infantry, under the command of Lieutenant Colonel Glenn H. Gardner, was fighting on Christmas Day alongside the armored infantry and tanks of CCB. By the end of the day, the battalion had reached

THE ROAD TO BASTOGNE   99

Three rifle companies made up each of the Fourth Armored Division's three armored infantry battalions. Losses among the division's armored infantry were always very high. This same situation would plague all of the U.S. Army's armored divisions in World War II. On a snow-covered road in the Ardennes, an M-3 half-track is flanked by a long column of marching infantrymen. *National Archives*

Other major elements of the Fourth Armored Division included its mechanized cavalry squadron, armed with M-5 light tanks and M-8 armored cars, an engineer battalion, and the division trains (supply services). Two American M-8 armored cars patrol the Ardennes. *National Archives*

the woods near the village of Hompre, some 4,000 yards from the Bastogne perimeter. A lieutenant and a four-man patrol from the 2nd Battalion managed to sneak through German lines to reach a Bastogne outpost in the early-morning darkness of December 26. CCR, on the left flank of CCB, had beaten it into Bastogne.

CCR was ordered to move from the eastern flank of CCA to the western flank of CCB. Its commander had selected his own route, to avoid destroyed bridges, and an assembly area was designated southwest of the village of

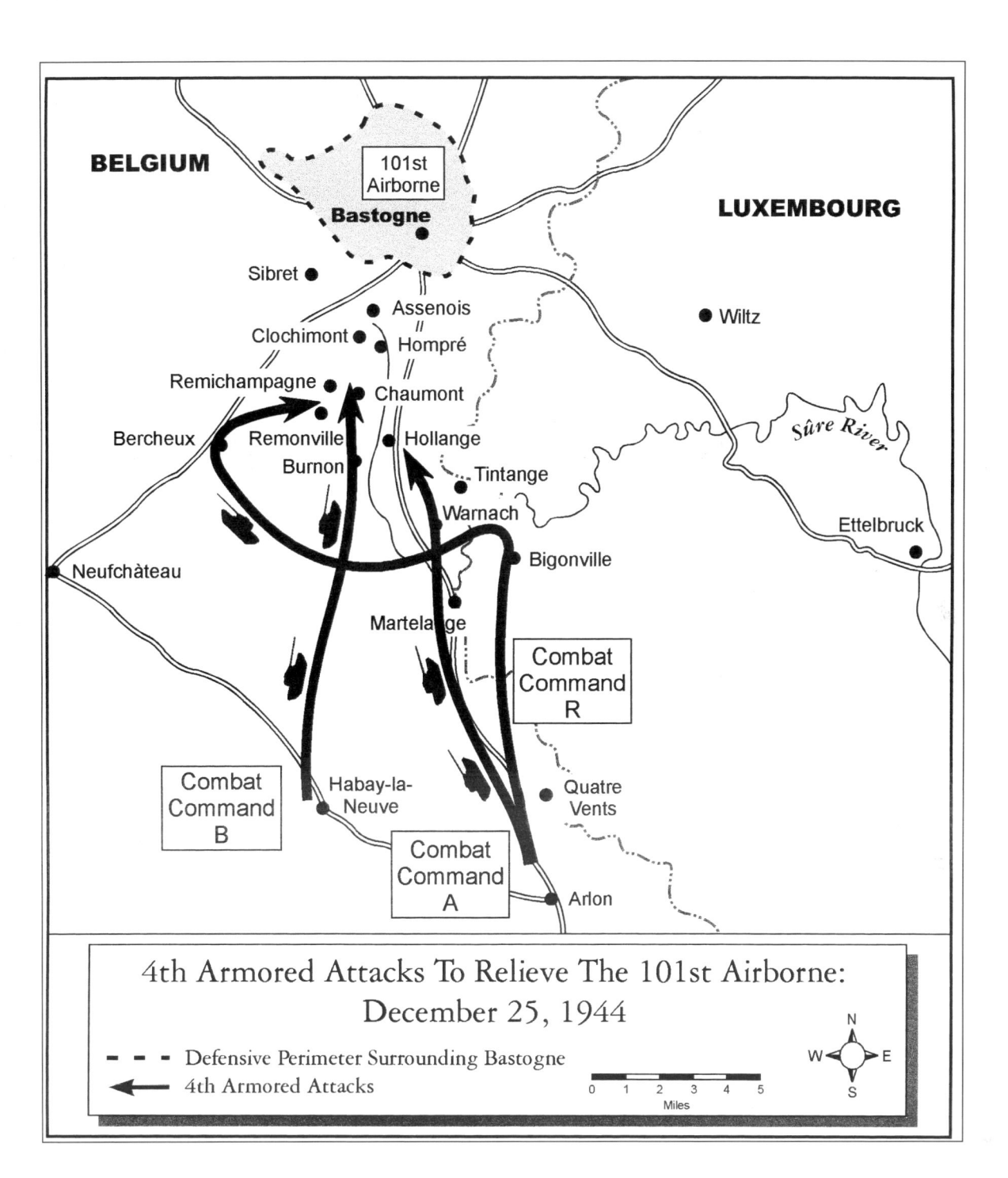

### 4th Armored Attacks To Relieve The 101st Airborne: December 25, 1944

- - - Defensive Perimeter Surrounding Bastogne
← 4th Armored Attacks

Bercheux on the Neufchâteau-Bastogne road. It was here that the men and equipment of the CCR would gather before heading toward Bastogne at dawn on Christmas Day. A big concern was the lack of information on German strength or dispositions along the 16-mile stretch of road that lay ahead of CCR.

Leading the advance toward Bastogne was the 37th Tank Battalion and the 53d Armored Infantry Battalion. The tank battalion was under the command of Lieutenant Colonel Creighton W. Abrams, nicknamed "Abe" by his tankers. The armored infantry battalion was under the command of Lieutenant Colonel George Jaques, nicknamed "Jigger Jakes" by his men. Support for these two leading units came from the self-propelled guns of the 94th Armored Field Artillery Battalion, and a battery of 155-millimeter howitzers from the 177th Field Artillery Battalion.

Bastogne could be reached from the south by two main approaches, on the right the Arlon-Bastogne road, on the left the Neufchâteau-Bastogne road. Two American soldiers inspect a knocked-out German Panther medium tank. *National Archives*

A mile and a half up the road from Bercheux stood the village of Vaux-lezRosieres. Beyond Vaux-lezRosieres was the German-occupied village of Remoiville. After some hard fighting, Remoiville was taken. The light tanks in the advance guard of CCR moved on, but had advanced only a few hundred yards by the end of Christmas Day. At Remoiville, CCR had come abreast of CCB on its right. Gaffey was still expecting CCB to make the breakthrough to Bastogne, now that CCR was guarding its west flank.

On Christmas night, Colonel Blanchard and the other officers of CCR gathered over a map that had just arrived by air courier. The map showed the disposition of the 101st Airborne Division within the Bastogne perimeter and a rough estimate of the German order of battle as it faced in toward Bastogne and out toward the Fourth Armored Division. Blan-

The problem facing the III Corps was not the simple one of gaining access to Bastogne or of restoring physical contact with the forces within it. The problem was how to restore and maintain a permanent corridor into the city; and how to jar the surrounding enemy loose so that Bastogne and its road net could be used by the Third Army as a base for further operations to the north and northeast. American soldiers string telephone line over an abandoned and snow-covered German Tiger II tank. *National Archives*

chard gave his plan for attack toward Bastogne on the next day. The plan called for an advance through Remichampagne (1 1/2 miles from Remoiville). If this plan succeeded, CCR would move on to the village of Clochimont.

At Clochimont, it was expected that CCR would either run into the German main line of defenses or face a serious counterattack. When CCR advance elements reached the outskirts of Clochimont, they began to move with great caution. Tanks and infantry were moved out on either side of the main column to provide flank protection in case of a German counterattack. Abrams sent one tank company northward hoping to draw fire from and uncover the next enemy position. A second objective was to uncover enemy positions in the village of Assenois, straight to his front, or Sibret, the objective assigned by Blanchard on the Bastogne highway.

Orders from the commanding officer of CCR specified that the village of Sibret be taken before moving on to Assenois. Abrams had information indicating that Sibret was heavily defended. Having no more than 20 medium tanks left within his battalion, Abrams was reluctant to risk losing them in an attempt to take Sibret and then have nothing left to continue the advance on to Bastogne. The 53rd Armored Infantry Battalion, already weakened by previous conflicts, was, like Abrams' 37th

Patton, a veteran tanker from World War I, prescribed the tactics to be used by the Fourth Armored Division in its attack toward Bastogne. He also ordered that the new, modified M-4 Sherman medium tank with heavier armor, the so-called Jumbo, be put in the lead when available. This brand new Jumbo is just off the assembly line. Turret armor on the Jumbo was 6 inches thick on the front, sides, and rear. The front of the Jumbo's hull was 4 inches thick, the hull side's were 3 inches thick. *Patton Museum*

THE ROAD TO BASTOGNE 103

Visibility was poor and the ground snow-covered when tanks of the Fourth Armored Division began their attack toward Bastogne on the morning of December 22. Both CCA and CCB of the division soon ran into various difficulties that slowed down their progress. To make up lost time, Patton ordered the advance to be continued through the night "to relieve Bastogne." On the rear deck of an American M-4 Sherman tank, a squad of infantry rides with weapons at the ready as the vehicle enters a small village. *National Archives*

The XIX TAC assisted the Fourth Armored Division in clearing a path for itself through German defenses. Due to the poor flying conditions, air support for the division was extremely limited. However, when available, American fighter-bombers took a heavy toll on enemy forces. The ground crew of a twin-engine Lockheed P-38 Lighting fighter prepares it for its next mission. *Real War Photos*

104    PATTON AND THE BATTLE OF THE BULGE

As the CCs of the Fourth Armored Division continued to push though German defenses to reach Bastogne, it was becoming painfully clear that the division was losing too many tanks to German antitank weapons. The decision was made on December 24 to employ infantry to lead the Fourth Armored Division's advance to Bastogne. Infantry battalions were transferred in from nearby infantry divisions to supplement the organic armored infantry of the armored division. Heading off into the Ardennes woods is a long column of American infantry. *Real War Photos*

Tank Battalion, short 230 men. Abrams and Jaques, the battalion commanders, decided to modify Blanchard's orders and dash through the village of Assenois straight on to Bastogne. They contacted Patton by radio to request his permission to change plans; Patton readily gave his permission and urged them on. Abrams quickly began to pull together the resources of CCR with artillery support from CCB on its right flank for an attack on Assenois. As the tanks and armored infantry of CCR began their advance, 13 batteries of artillery opened fire on the German defenders of the village. A colorful and vivid description of that attack, and the subsequent breakthrough to Bastogne by CCR can be found in the Fourth Armored Division's official history. It starts:

"The final assault was launched from the far edge of Assenois, the last village before Bastogne. In the lead was Company C of the 37th Tank Battalion, followed by Company C of the 53d Armored Infantry Battalion. Lieutenant Colonel Creighton W. Abrams, then commander of the 37th Tank Battalion, clinched a cold cigar in the corner of his mouth and said, 'We're going in to those people now.' With that, he swept his arm forward and the charge was on.

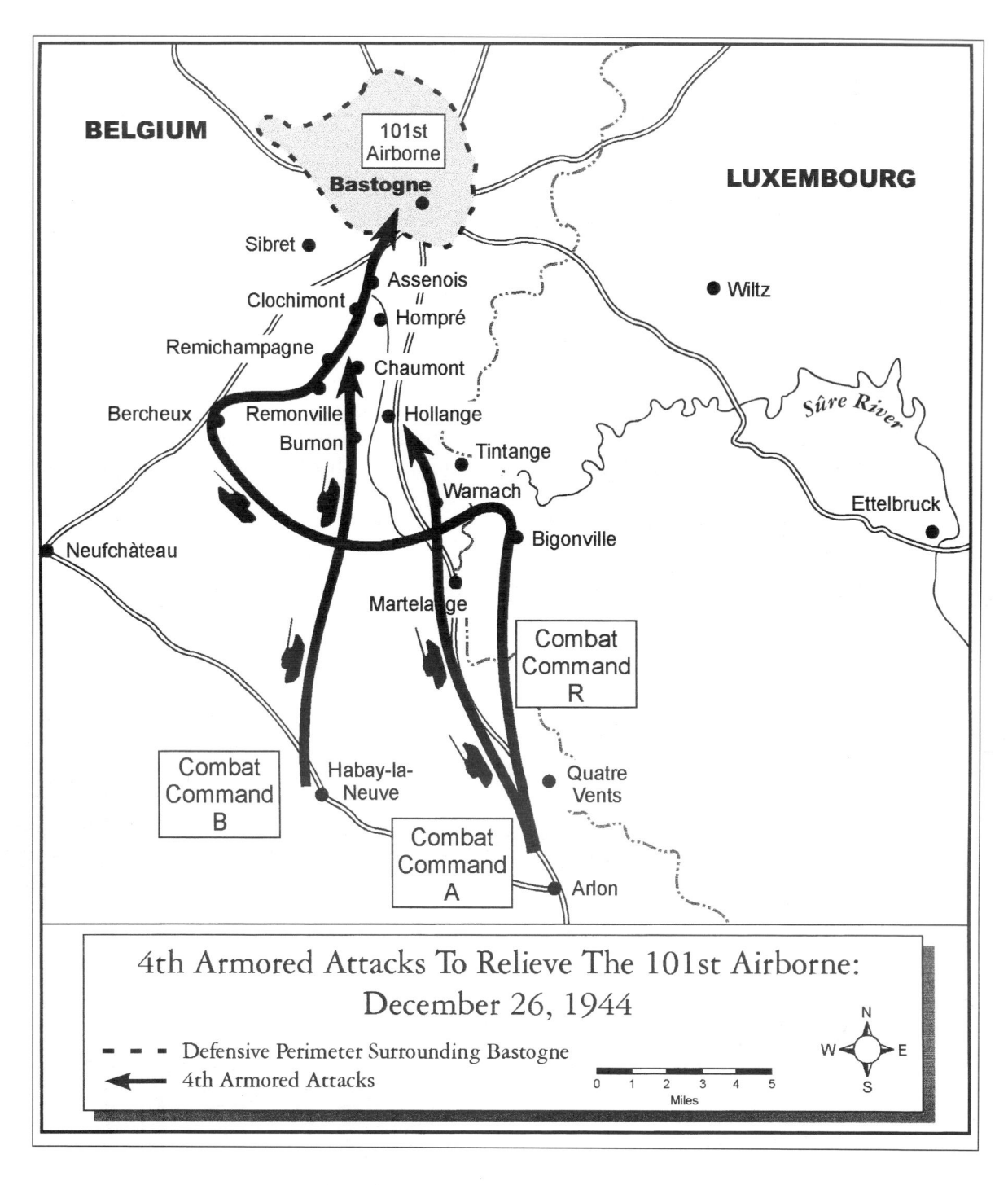

### 4th Armored Attacks To Relieve The 101st Airborne: December 26, 1944

- - - Defensive Perimeter Surrounding Bastogne
← 4th Armored Attacks

"The command tank of Company C, 37th Tank Battalion, moved out first. In the turret was First Lieutenant Charles Boggess, Jr. 'The Germans had these two little towns of Clochimont and Assenois on the secondary road we were using to get to Bastogne,' Lieutenant Boggess recalled. 'Beyond Assenois the road ran up a ridge through heavy woods. There were lots of Germans there, too. We were going through fast, all guns firing, straight up that road to bust through before they had time to get set. I thought of a lot of things as we took off. I thought of whether the road would be mined, whether the bridge in Assenois would be blown, whether they would be ready at their antitank guns. Then we charged, and I didn't have any time to wonder.'

"Meanwhile, four American artillery battalions were slamming barrages into enemy-held Assenois and the edge of the woods

The German XLVII Panzer Corps commander became worried about a relief column from Patton's III Corps pushing through his lines into Bastogne on the evening of Christmas Day. He requested additional reinforcements and wanted to call off the attacks on Bastogne. The German Fifth Army had no more reinforcement to commit. Reviewing a map are Patton and Major General Troy H. Middleton, commander of Patton's VIII Corps during the fighting in the Ardennes. *Patton Museum*

my left brake locked and the tank turned up a road we didn't want to go. So I just stopped her, backed her up and went on again.'

"The armored infantry was also in the thick of the fighting, and one of the infantrymen distinguished himself gallantly enough to become the third Congressional Medal of Honor winner in the Fourth Armored Division. He was Private James Hendrix, a 19-year-old rifleman with Company C, 53d Armored Infantry Battalion.

"His citation read: 'Private Hendrix dismounted and advanced upon two 88-millimeter gun crews, and by the ferocity of his actions

beyond it. The 22nd, 66th, and 94th Armored Artillery Battalions of the 4th Armored dropped in 105-millimeter shells, and a supporting battalion lobbed 155-millimeter howitzer rounds.

"Under the artillery support, Lieutenant Boggess' medium tank advanced through shell bursts from the enemy positions. The ground pitched and houses spilled into the street, but the undaunted American force kept going. 'I used the 75 (75-millimeter main gun) like a machine gun,' said Lieutenant Boggess' gunner, Corporal Milton Dickerman. 'Murphy (Private James, the loader) was plenty busy throwing in the shells. We shot 21 rounds in a few minutes and I don't know how much machine gun stuff. As we got to Assenois an antitank gun in a half-track fired at us. The shell hit the road in front of the tank and threw dirt all over. I got the half-track in my sights and hit it with high explosive. It blew up.'

"Dirt from the enemy shell burst had smeared the driver's periscope. 'I made out okay, although I couldn't see very good,' explained Private Hubert Smith. 'I sort of guessed at the road. I had a little trouble when

The German XLVII Panzer Corps commander was convinced that with enough reinforcements, he could finally take Bastogne once and for all. He would be sadly disappointed in that belief. Despite numerous regimental-size attacks beginning on Christmas Eve and running through Christmas Day, the Germans achieved little or no success. The American advantage of interior lines clearly served to complicate German attempts to coordinate their efforts. The crew of an American 57-millimeter antitank gun guards a snow-covered road in the Ardennes. *Patton Museum*

THE ROAD TO BASTOGNE 107

German minefields also played an important part in delaying the advance of the Fourth Armored Division toward Bastogne. Finding and removing German mines was a time-consuming and dangerous job, especially since it was standard German practice to defend the approaches to their regular minefields with a covering party of four or five men with one or two light machine guns. These two American M-4 Sherman medium tanks were caught in a German minefield. The vehicle on the right had its onboard ammunition explode, resulting in its entire side hull armor being peeled back like a banana. *Patton Museum*

compelled the German gun crews first to take cover and then surrender.'

"Hendrix, a red-haired, freckle-faced farm boy from Arkansas, later explained, 'We ran up on them yelling 'come out' but they wouldn't. One poked his head out of a foxhole and I shot him through the neck. I got closer and hit another on the head with the butt of my M-l. He had American matches on him. Others came out then with their hands up.'

"The citation continues: "Later in the attack this fearless soldier again left his vehicle voluntarily to aid two wounded soldiers threatened by enemy machine gun fire. Effectively silencing two enemy machine guns, he held off the enemy by his own fire until the wounded men were evacuated.'

"'I just shot at the machine guns like all the 50s on the half-tracks were doing,' Hendrix said. 'A half-track had been hit pretty bad and these fellows were wounded and lying in a ditch. Machine gun fire was mostly toward them, but some bullets were coming my way.'

"Continuing the attack, Hendrix again endangered himself when he ran to aid still another soldier who was trapped in a burning half-track. Braving enemy sniper fire and exploding mines and ammunition in the vehicle, he pulled the wounded man from the conflagration and extinguished his flaming clothing with his own body.

The Germans employed about 40 different types of antitank mines during World War II. The most widely used were four versions of an antitank mine designated Tellermines. They had an average diameter of about 12 inches and were armed with roughly 12 pounds of TNT. It normally took a minimum pressure of 495 pounds to set the Tellermines off. This American soldier had recovered several Tellermines as well as a couple of Panzerfausts and a single German stick grenade from the battlefield. *National Archives*

108   PATTON AND THE BATTLE OF THE BULGE

A two-man U.S. Army mine-sweeping team checks the side of a snow-covered Ardennes road. They are using an electrical mine detector designated by the Army as detector set SCR-625. A trained detector operator could sweep a nine-foot front for about 20 minutes before being relieved by his partner. Longer periods of sweeping would cause operator fatigue and result in incomplete sweeping. *National Archives*

"Hendrix explained it so: 'A grenade exploded between his legs and everybody else got out. But he was hollering for help. I pulled at him and got him out on the road, but he was burned bad. I tried to find water to put out the fire, but the water cans were full of bullet holes, so I beat out the flames as best I could. He died later.'

"The four lead tanks in Boggess' column drew ahead as the half-tracks were slowed by German shells and debris. The tankers rolled along, sweeping the wooded ridge with machine-gun fire. Finally, they burst through the German defenses and into the 101st Airborne perimeter.

"Lieutenant Boggess ordered the roaring Sherman tank down to a canter. In the open fields beyond the pines he saw red, yellow, and blue supply parachutes spilled over the snow like confetti. Some of the colored chutes, caught in the tall pines, indicated where ammunition, food, and medicine had been dropped to the besieged troops. The column halted.

"Standing up in his turret, Lieutenant Boggess shouted, "Come here, come on out," to khaki-clad figures in foxholes. 'This is the 4th Armored.' There was no answer. Helmeted heads peered suspiciously over carbine sights. The lieutenant shouted again. A lone figure

THE ROAD TO BASTOGNE 109

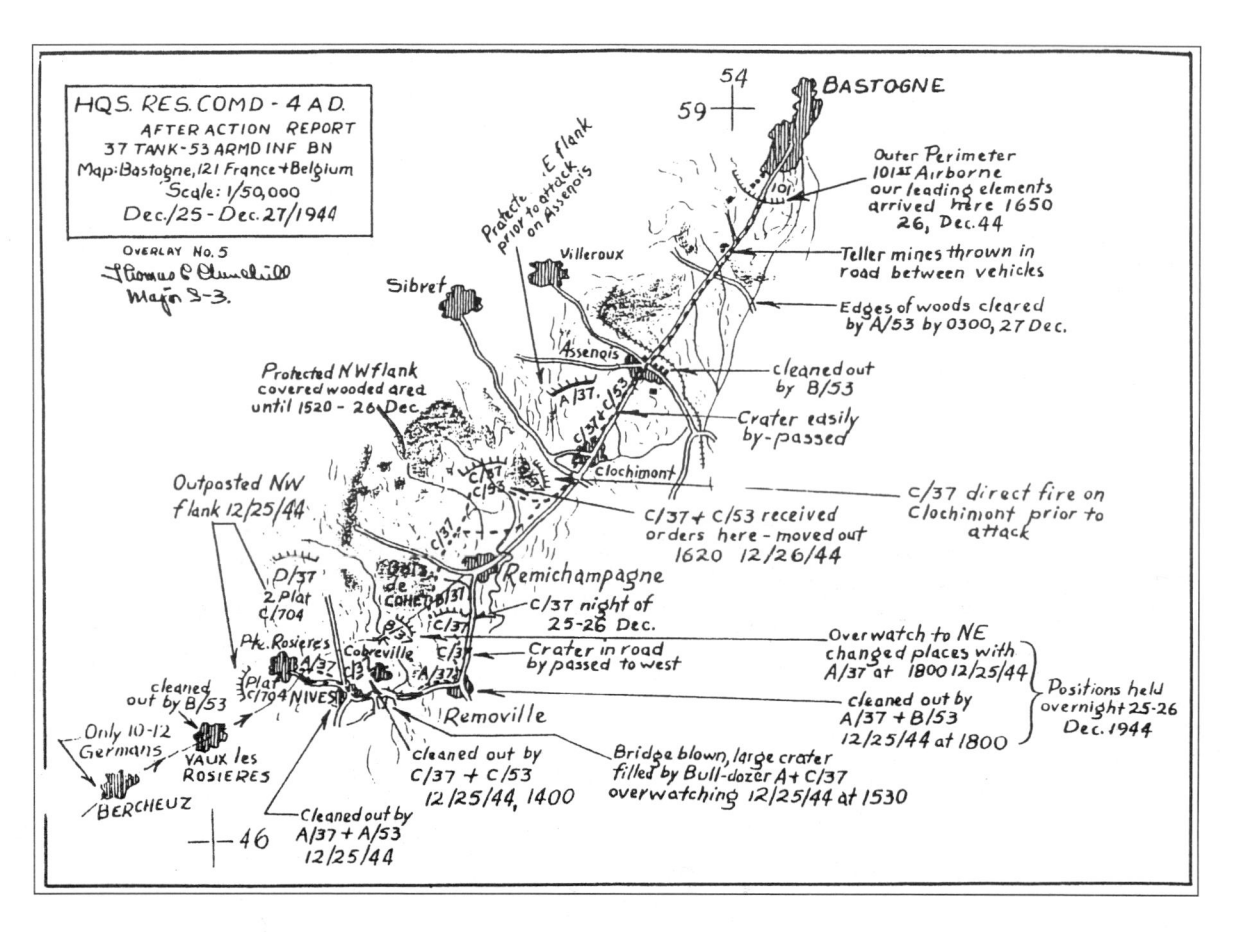

The U.S. Army designed and built large steel mine rollers that could detonate buried enemy mines without damage to the equipment itself. Due to the massive size and bulk of the mine rollers, they were fitted to the front of M-4 Sherman tank recovery vehicles. *National Archives*

strode forward. Lieutenant Boggess watched him carefully.

"'I'm Lieutenant Webster of the 326th Engineers, 101st Airborne Division,' the approaching figure called. 'Glad to see you.' The time was 4:45 p.m., December 26. The gap behind the four front-running tanks had, however, given the Germans a chance to lob mines onto the road. One half-track struck a mine and was destroyed. Infantrymen ran forward against bazooka and machine-gun fire to clear the mines, but three more half-tracks were blown up. Fighting mostly on foot, the rest of the column reached the trapped troops."

Bastogne was, however, still not secure. The Germans were not ready to give up without a stiff fight. Of the nine roads and two rail lines running into the town, only the Fourth Armored Division corridor was linked to the outside world.

On December 26 Patton wrote in his notes: "Combat Command A, 9th Armored Division, serving with 10th Armored Division in XII Corps joined to Fourth Armored Division this

CCR of the Fourth Armored Division had been tasked with the capture of a nearby village, instead of entering Bastogne. This fact did not sit well with the battalion commanders of CCR. They decided on their own that it made more sense for their force to break into Bastogne, since it was closer than CCB. After conferring with Patton by radio, they were given permission to enter Bastogne. American tankers carefully remove a wounded crewman from an M-5 light tank. *National Archives*

On December 26, CCR of the Fourth Armored Division managed to fight its way to within a couple of miles of Bastogne, with the help of the XIX TAC. It was at this point that it would soon run into the rear of the German forces besieging Bastogne. Despite the closeness of CCR to Bastogne, the original plans for the relief of the town still called for CCB of the Fourth Armored Division to do the honors of breaking the German siege. A captured German armored half-track has been pressed into U.S. Army service. *National Archives*

On the road to Bastogne, the relief column from CCR of the Fourth Armored Division had to pass through the German-held village of Assenois, whose defenders put up a stiff fight. It took almost all of the relief column's armored infantry to subdue the village's defenders. American soldiers in snowsuits have captured a number of German soldiers. *National Archives*

The attack into Bastogne by CCR of the Fourth Armored Division was led by M-4 Sherman medium tanks, followed by M-3 half-tracks carrying armored infantry. A long column of whitewashed American M-4 Sherman tanks, armed with a high-velocity 76-millimeter gun, moves along a snow-covered road. *National Archives*

morning and attacks west of CCR (Colonel Blanchard) Fourth Armored Division.

"Colonel Blanchard's CCR by a very daring attack entered Bastogne (at) 1645 with one battalion of armored infantry and one battalion of tanks. We took in 40 truckloads of supplies that night, thus reopening the supply route. Also, 22 ambulances with a total of 652 wounded were evacuated; the first night 224 went out and the remaining were evacuated the next morning.

"The total time from the moment when the Fourth Armored Division left the Saarbrucken sector to the taking of Bastogne was seven days; the distance covered was 120 miles; the distances gained by combat during four days was 16 miles. In addition to the Fourth Armored Division, the 318th Infantry (less 3rd

THE ROAD TO BASTOGNE 113

Five M-4 Sherman medium tanks and a single half-track dashed through the town of Assenois and made for the Bastogne perimeter. As they approached Bastogne, the single half-track struck a mine and was put out of action. The remaining five American tanks pressed on. This destroyed American M-4 Sherman tank had its onboard ammunition explode, as can be seen in the buckled lower hull plates. *Patton Museum*

Battalion) of the 80th Division and Combat Command A of the 9th Armored Division should be given special credit for the penetration into Bastogne.

"The 6th Armored Division closed on Luxembourg. The 87th Infantry and 17th Airborne and 11th Armored Divisions are near Reims in SHAEF Reserve. The Third Army requested their assignment."

Shortly after CCR of the Fourth Armored Division managed to link up with the defenders inside Bastogne. Patton wrote to Gaffey:

"The outstanding celerity of your movement and the unremitting, vicious, and skillful manner in which you pushed the attack terminating at the end of four days and four nights of incessant battle in the relief of Bastogne, constitute one of the finest chapters in the glorious history of the United States Army."

Patton also wrote to his wife, that:

"The relief of Bastogne is the most brilliant operation we have thus far performed and is in my opinion the outstanding achievement of this war."

On December 26 tankers in the lead tank of the relief column from CCR of the Fourth Armored Division saw some engineers in friendly uniforms preparing to assault a German pillbox near the highway into Bastogne. These were men from the 326th Airborne Engineer Battalion, and it marked the first contact between CCR and the defenders of Bastogne. Patton and Brigadier General Anthony C. McAuliffe of the 101st Airborne Division confer after the siege of Bastogne was lifted. McAuliffe commanded the forces within Bastogne during the German siege. *Patton Museum*

Light German probing attacks against Bastogne continued on December 27 and 28, but the XLVII Panzer Corps was becoming more defensively oriented. With the 101st Airborne Division still holding on to Bastogne, it forced the Fifth Panzer Army's supply columns to make long detours. An abandoned German unarmored half-track in the Ardennes had been towing a 105-millimeter howitzer. *National Archives*

## Chapter Four

# Clearing the Bastogne Area

When CCR of the Fourth Armored Division reached the American defensive perimeter around Bastogne on December 26, the contact between the 101st Airborne Division and Millikin's III Corps was tentative at best. The road between Assenois-Bastogne was still subject to enemy harassing fire. The two main highways east and west of the Assenois-Bastogne corridor were still held by Brandenberger's Seventh Army. Access to Bastogne by Millikin's III Corps would have to be gained by widening the breach punched through German lines by CCR and securing the Arlon-Bastogne highway. The segment of the main road between Neufchâteau-Assenois would also have to be cleared to prevent the Germans from rushing in with armored units.

The bulk of Gaffey's Fourth Armored Division still lay east of Assenois along the Arlon-Bastogne road. Patton assigned the 9th Armored Division CCA to Gaffey on the morning of December 26 for an attack along the left flank of CCR to clear the villages along the Neufchâteau-Bastogne highway.

All vehicles traveling in and out of Bastogne on December 26 had to be escorted. CCR was occupied in providing convoy protection. CCA and CCB of the Fourth Armored Division continued to push slowly toward Bastogne. On the morning of December 26, CCB attacked the German-defended village of Hompre (5 miles south of Bastogne). By nightfall, patrols from CCB had reached the 101st Airborne Division's defensive perimeter. CCA was having a much harder time getting near Bastogne. Ten miles south of Bastogne, the Americans had to destroy the village of Sainlez in order to flush the Germans out of hiding. When the German defenders of Sainlez fled the village, they moved east and struck the 1st Battalion of the 318th Infantry Battalion (attached to CCA), which had just cleared the nearby village of Livarchamps. The fighting in Livarchamps continued through the night and resulted in heavy

Even as American convoys entered Bastogne by way of Assenois, the two main roads east and west of the Assenois corridor were still barred by elements of the German Seventh Army. To keep the road linking the defenders of Bastogne with Patton's III Corps open, the breach in German lines would have to be widened. American soldiers take cover behind an M-4 Sherman medium tank during the fighting in the Ardennes. *Real War Photos*

When tanks of CCR of the Fourth Armored Division first reached the Bastogne perimeter on the afternoon of December 26, the contact between its defenders and the III Corps of Patton's Third Army was not very secure. The only way to get supply trucks in and out of Bastogne was by armed convoys. An American M-5 light tank leads a truck supply column toward Bastogne. *Patton Museum*

American casualties. Frostbite cases among the infantrymen of CCA soon equaled the unit's battle losses.

As CCA and CCB and their attached formations continued to push forward to Bastogne, the American defensive perimeter around the town remained unusually quiet. Major General Maxwell Taylor, commander of the 101st Airborne Division, entered the town on December 27 to reassume his command. He also took the time to congratulate his subordinate, Brigadier General Anthony McAuliffe, on doing such an outstanding job in his absence.

A large number of supply trucks and replacements for the 101st Airborne Division followed Taylor into Bastogne. A medical collecting company arrived to move the casualties back to hospitals. By noon on December 28, the last ambulance had left the town. December 28 also marked the return of winter's full fury and the end of five days of clear weather over the Ardennes. After December 27, the poor weather

Patton knew that widening the corridor into Bastogne carved open by CCR of the Fourth Armored Division was only part of the solution. To truly secure the relief of Bastogne, Patton's III Corps would have to clear the Arlon to Bastogne road, as well as the Neufchâteau to Assenois road. It would only be a matter of time before the Germans would launch large-scale counterattacks to seal off the opening into Bastogne. German officers confer before their next mission. *National Archives*

allowed the XIX TAC to put aircraft into the air only sporadically. These brief periods of flying time still proved very important to Third Army operations. The Germans saw the return of bad weather as an opportunity to even the odds and began bringing in additional units for a new offensive aimed at Bastogne.

Excerpts from a German newspaper article dated January 5, 1945, describe the American reliance on air superiority during the fighting in the Ardennes:

"The German counterthrust has demonstrated to what a high degree the Anglo-Amer-

As CCR of the Fourth Armored Division shepherded trucks on the Assenois road into Bastogne, its sister units, CCB and CCA, continued to push north toward Bastogne. American M-4 Sherman medium tanks, along with infantry, push through a snow-covered Ardennes Forest. *National Archives*

118   PATTON AND THE BATTLE OF THE BULGE

On December 27 CCB of the Fourth Armored Division launched an attack from west of the village of Hompre against troops of the 15th Panzer Grenadier Division. By nightfall of December 27, its patrols had reached the 101st Airborne Division's defensive perimeter around Bastogne. American soldiers are pictured passing a German roadblock. *National Archives*

ican combat forces are tied up with their air combat forces and how without the protection of their bombers and fighters—which were hampered at the beginning of the offensive by unfavorable weather conditions—they are unable to offer any worthwhile resistance.

"The enemy, who had thus been forced into hard straits, waited most eagerly for the chance to use his air forces. And sure enough, as the weather cleared, American fighter-bombers and fighters immediately appeared over the Ardennes and in the earliest hours of

CCA of the Fourth Armored Division entered Bastogne on the night of December 30. It quickly took up defensive positions within the defensive perimeter set up by the 101st Airborne Division and its supporting units. Pictured is the crew of an American .30-caliber (air-cooled) machine gun in a defensive trench. *National Archives*

CLEARING THE BASTOGNE AREA 119

With the partial relief of Bastogne by Patton's III Corps at the end of December, both sides took stock of the situation. Hitler decided that Bastogne had to be taken as quickly as possible. He therefore ordered every available division to concentrate around Bastogne for a major attack. American soldiers are pictured in the Ardennes trying on some locally made snowsuits. *National Archives*

the morning sought, over the close terrain of the front, the packs of German tanks and their communications routes. The Americans were not yet able to make use of their heavy bombers, since area bombing, with the troops mixed together as they were, would have endangered their own forces."

By the morning of December 28, Patton's III Corps had noticed that the German units in their path were putting up more of a fight. Anticipating Eisenhower's impatience with the slow progress of the Third Army's drive to clear the area around Bastogne, Patton had twice called his boss to apologize. In addition, Patton had already ordered his staff to work on plans for a prompt redirection of the Third Army attack. The impetus for this redirection of forces came from a set of three plans presented on December 27 by Lieutenant General J. Lawton Collins, commander of the VII Corps of the First Army. Two of Collins' plans called for merging with Patton in the Bastogne area. The third plan specified as the objective the Belgian village of St. Vith, about 25 miles northeast of Bastogne.

Collins' proposed plans brought home an important issue for the American commanders regarding German penetration in the Ardennes. The two best options were to cut off the German penetration close to its shoulders, or at its base. Patton argued that the German penetration in the Ardennes should be cut off at its base by Allied attacks from both the northern and southern flank. If this plan of action were adopted, Patton would move the Third Army northeast from Luxembourg City

120    PATTON AND THE BATTLE OF THE BULGE

As Hitler was ordering Bastogne to be taken at all costs, Eisenhower was rushing in reinforcements to launch his own attack to clear the entire area around Bastogne of German forces. A very large and bloody collision between two attacking forces was about to take place. Shown is a long column of American infantry marching to the front in the Ardennes. *National Archives*

toward the vicinity of Prum, a little over 10 miles inside Germany. At Prum, it could link up with the American First Army under Hodges, which was coming from the north. By joining together at Prum, the two American armies would effectively prevent the German forces in the Ardennes from pulling back behind the safety of the Siegfried Line. Hodges agreed with Patton's approach in principle, but felt that the roads in the area could not support the large armored force that would be needed to successfully achieve this objective.

Bradley, the 12th Army Group commander, believed that the combination of inhospitable terrain and weather would doom Patton's plan to certain failure. He was also concerned about the lack of reserves that Patton's plan would create for SHAEF. The 6th Army Group had already dangerously thinned its lines to help release the bulk of Patton's Third Army for battles in the Ardennes. On December 27, Bradley suggested to Eisenhower that the Third Army attack start from the Bastogne area and continue northeast toward St. Vith. Bradley took great pains to inform Eisenhower that this plan was not Patton's concept of an advance against the base of the German penetration—instead, it was clearly aimed at the shoulders of the German formation. Eisenhower accepted Bradley's suggestion, much to Patton's dismay. Montgomery, commander of the 21st Army Group, had also favored a two-pronged attack at the shoulders of the German penetration. He wanted to see the First Army, then under his command, link up with the Third Army at Houffalize, Belgium, 9 miles northeast of Bastogne. Despite these rebuffs, Patton still had plans to launch his XII Corps

German intelligence officers had quickly picked up evidence of the American attack preparations taking place. They accurately predicted that the 6th Armored Division (nicknamed the "Super Sixth") soon would appear between Patton's III and VIII Corps. The 6th Armored Division was transferred to the III Corps by Patton to replace the worn-out Fourth Armored Division, which had only 44 medium tanks left. An American soldier points to a large hole made in the turret of an M-4 Sherman tank by a German antitank gun. *National Archives*

A German intelligence report of December 27 read: "It is expected that the units of the Third Army, under the energetic leadership of General Patton, will make strong attacks against our south flank." Pictured together shaking hands are Patton and Lieutenant General William H. Simpson, commander of the American Ninth Army. *Patton Museum*

in the direction of Prum, Germany if the opportunity arose. (The XII Corps was located on the south flank of the III Corps and was commanded by Major General Manton S. Eddy.)

On December 28, Eisenhower added the American 11th Armored Division, and the 87th Infantry Division to Bradley's 12th Army Group. Both divisions came from the reformed SHAEF reserves. Bradley, in turn, informed Patton that the only reinforcements he could use were his VIII Corps, advancing from the center of the Ardennes toward Bastogne. (After the initial German attack on December 16, and prior to December 28, the VIII Corps had under its control only the units within Bastogne, remnants of the 28th Infantry Division, and an assortment of other smaller units.)

On the night of December 28, Patton met with the VIII and III Corps commanders to lay out the plans for continuation of the new Third Army attack. Middleton's VIII Corps would attack from west of Bastogne on the morning of December 30. Its assigned objective was the high ground and road network just south of Houffalize. The next day Millikin's III Corps, moving up from the south, would begin advancing in a northeast direction toward St. Vith. (St. Vith had passed into German hands on December 21, Houffalize fell to the Germans on December 22.)

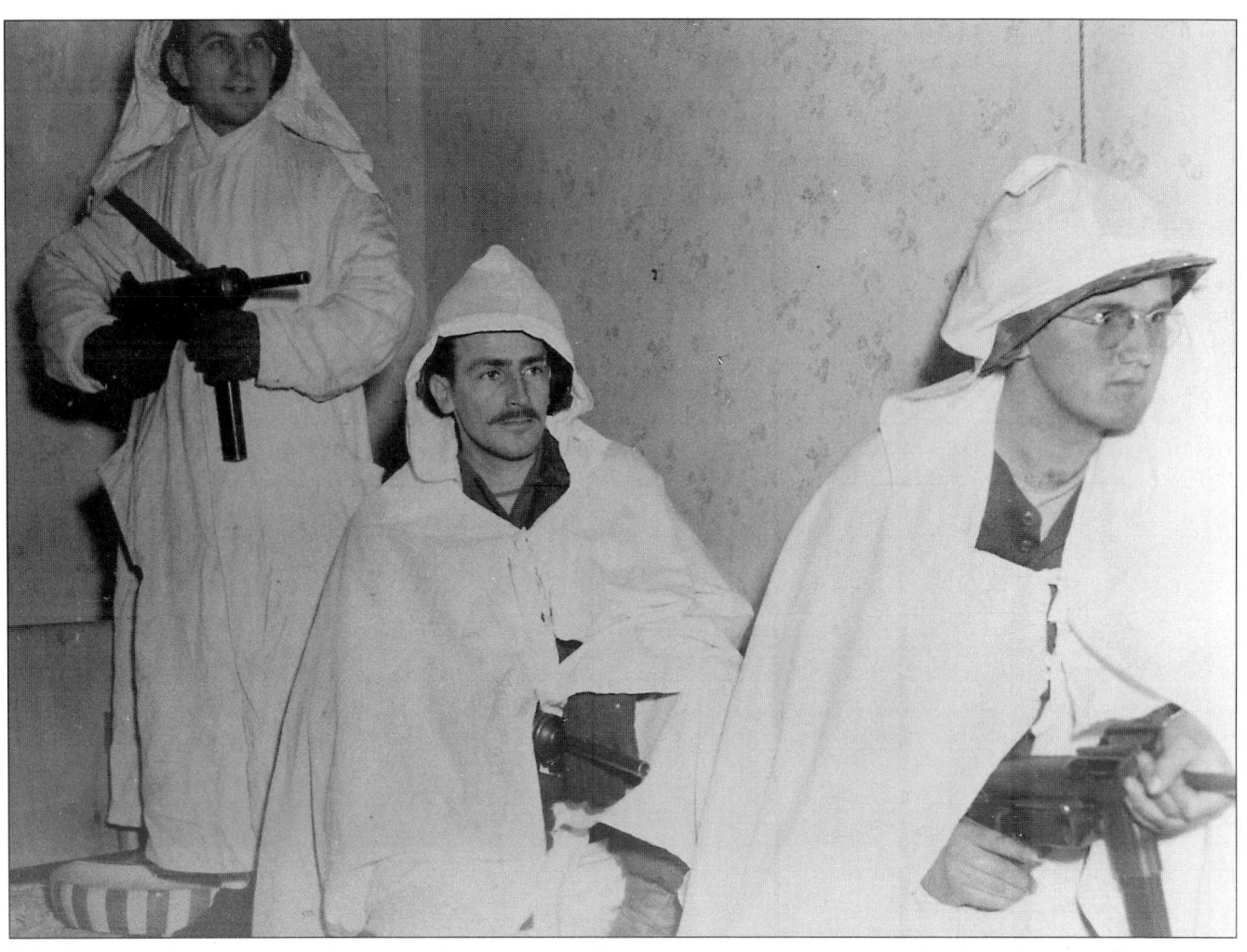

Within 24 hours, the German view changed regarding the American intentions. The Germans issued a revised report that indicated that the American First Army was having difficulty regrouping and still showed defensive tendencies; therefore, even though the Third Army was in position to attack, it probably would not attack alone. Pictured are three American soldiers armed with the M-3 submachine gun and wearing crude snowsuits. *National Archives*

### Widening the Path to Bastogne

The 9th Armored Division CCA received its orders on December 26. CCA was to push forward on the left flank of CCR of the Fourth Armored Division and attack in the direction of Sibret. There was more at stake than defending the corridor opened by CCR into Bastogne, Middleton had already begun making plans for his VIII Corps to join the Third Army attack beyond Bastogne. The one thing that the VIII Corps commander wanted to avoid was having to push his divisions through Bastogne's narrow streets. He therefore convinced Bradley and Patton that the VIII Corps should start its advance from a line of departure west of Bastogne. This tactic required that the entire Neufchâteau-Bastogne road be opened and the enemy driven back to the northwest.

When CCA started down the Neufchâteau road to Sibret on the morning of December 26, it had little or no information on enemy units in its path. (This was a serious problem for both sides throughout the campaign.) The CCA commander, Colonel Thomas L. Harrold, therefore divided his command into two task forces, "Collins" and "Karsteter." Task Force Collins was ordered to take Sibret. Task Force Karsteter was ordered to take the nearby village of Villeroux. Both villages were considered key defensive positions to the Germans around Bastogne, since they overlooked the Neufchâteau-Bastogne road.

Task Force Collins rushed into Sibret with all guns blazing on the morning of December 27. The village fell that night after heavy fighting. In a futile effort to retake Sibret, the

Germans launched counterattacks on the mornings of December 28 and 29. On the morning of December 29, Task Force Collins pushed on to the nearby village of Chenogne, which it reached late that afternoon. Shortly after the task force arrived in Chenogne, German tanks destroyed four American tanks. Gunners were unable to spot the enemy tanks in the twilight, and the decision was made to wait for morning to mount an attack on the village. That night, the VIII Corps artillery "blew Chenogne apart" to open a path for the attack. When the artillery barrage hit Chenogne, German tanks within the village withdrew to a safe area, but rushed back in to defend when the American artillery barrage concluded.

Task Force Karsteter, which consisted of two medium tank companies, managed to reach the village of Villeroux on the evening of December 27 and waited while American artillery and fighter-bombers laid waste to the village and its defenders. The tanks of Task Force Karsteter were then sent in to Villeroux to finish off any survivors. The American task force then moved northward toward the nearby village of Senonchamps, the scene of hard fighting in previous days and an entrance

American intelligence agencies were having their own problems predicting what the Germans might do next. They had practically no knowledge of any German units except those already in contact with American forces. Two American soldiers are inspecting a small German armored half-track abandoned in the Ardennes. The crudely painted American identification stars on the vehicle were done by the Germans to mislead enemy troops about its origins. *National Archives*

onto the main road running west from Bastogne to Marche.

As it left Villeroux, Task Force Karsteter came under heavy fire from the woods near the village of Bois de Fragotte. The Americans had encountered the main body of the 3rd Panzer Grenadier Division. Losses among the American armored infantry were very high. Four of the tanks from the task force ran the gauntlet of fire from the woods and entered Senonchamps, but the armored infantry was unable to follow. The losses sustained by the 9th Armored Division CCA in the three-day operation left it with a company and a half of infantry and only 38 light and medium tanks.

Task Force Collins was headed toward Chenogne on December 29, but it was not alone. In the confusion of battle, a small unit from the American 11th Armored CCB (known as Task Force Pat) had also made Chenogne its objective. On the way to Chenogne, Task Force Pat had the misfortune of running into elements of the Fuehrer Escort Brigade, and it withdrew after suffering heavy losses in men and equipment.

Poker, another Task Force of the 11th Armored Division CCB, was aiming for the village of Lavaselle, about 1 1/2 miles west of Chenogne. The surrounding terrain made Lavaselle inhospitable for tanks, so the task force commander decided to move on to the villages of Brul and Houmont, on high ground just to the north. There was a creek to cross with a single rickety bridge, but the tanks made it. The twin hamlets were defended only by a few German infantrymen and fell easily. As

American intelligence agencies did expect some type of German counterattack, but they believed it would come when bad weather would limit air activity. The weather did turn foul on December 28, and the word went out to American units: "Prepare for an armored counterattack—enemy tanks are in movement around Bastogne." An American soldier is inspecting a destroyed German Panther medium tank. *National Archives*

soon as the Germans realized what had happened, they bombarded the Americans with intense rocket and mortar fire from Lavaselle. Task Force Poker was on its own, well in front of the rest of the 11th Armored Division, waiting for the division's other task forces to pull abreast of its position at Chenogne.

The 11th Armored Division would continue its advance as part of Middleton's VIII Corps for three more bloody days of combat until replaced by the 17th Airborne Division on January 3. Once relieved, the 11th Armored Division was returned to SHAEF reserve. For a gain of only 4 miles, the division lost 220 killed and missing and 441 wounded during its few days in the Ardennes. In addition, the division lost 42 medium and 12 light tanks. The 87th Infantry Division, which entered into the fray at the same time as the 11th Armored Division as part of the VIII Corps advance, also suffered substantial losses in the battle to reach Bastogne from the west.

## The Two Attacks Collide

December 30 would dawn as an incredibly confusing day for both American and German soldiers fighting in the snow and ice around Bastogne. Almost every American advance was running into a German advance coming from the opposite direction. Both sides had begun a major offensive aimed at Bastogne and the open corridor that connected it to the Third Army at the same time.

An after-action report of Bradley's 12th Army Group described the situation around Bastogne at the end of December:

"Preoccupation with the key position of Bastogne dominated enemy strategy to such an

Patton and his senior commanders had decided to schedule their attack to clear the area around Bastogne on December 30. This date was firm insofar as the American Third Army was concerned. Pictured is a group of American infantry riding on, and walking beside, an M-4 Sherman medium tank in the Ardennes. *National Archives*

CLEARING THE BASTOGNE AREA 127

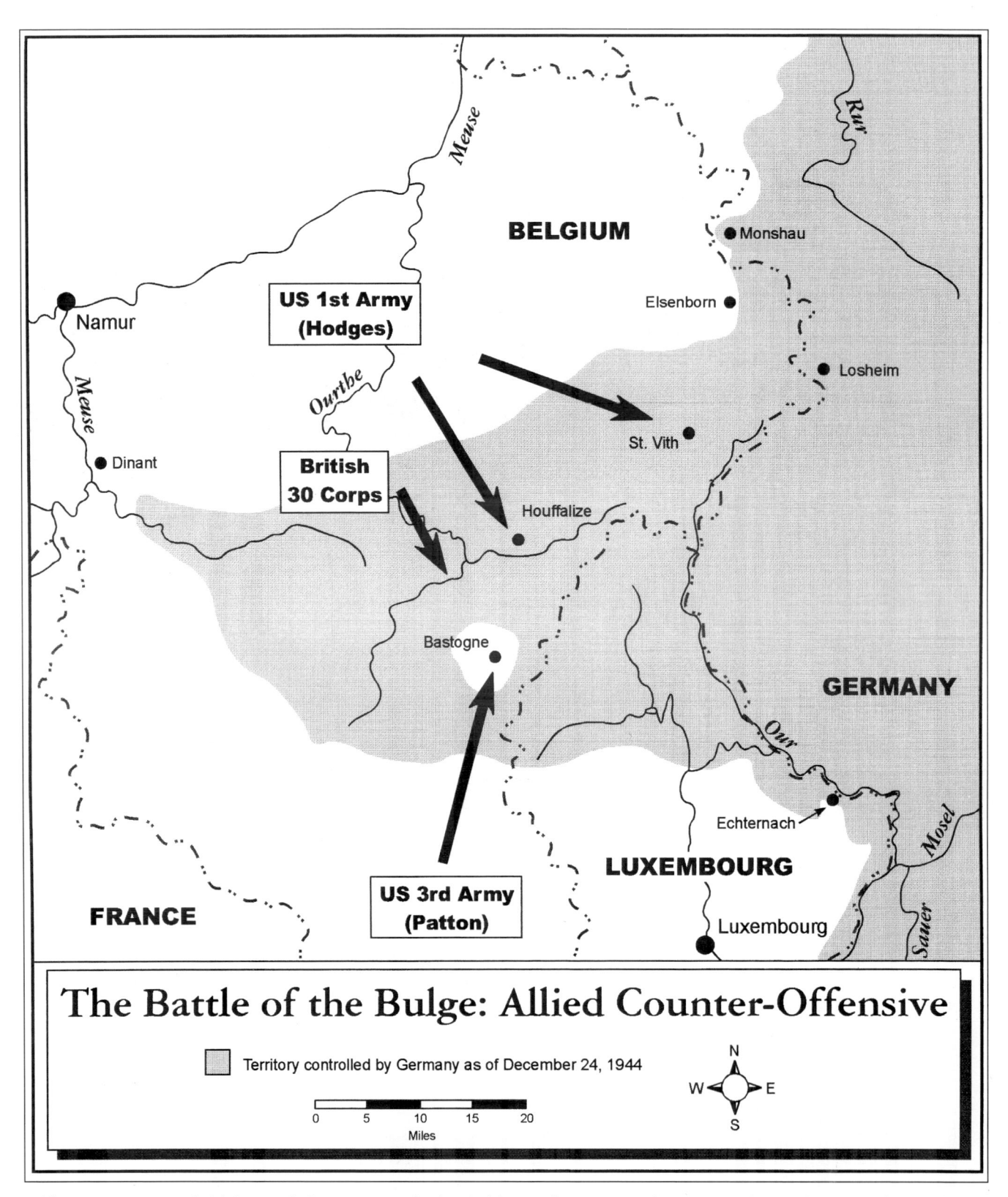

## The Battle of the Bulge: Allied Counter-Offensive

Territory controlled by Germany as of December 24, 1944

Middleton's VIII Corps was scheduled to provide the American spearhead on the left wing of Patton's army. The American 11th Armored Division, rushed over from England before finishing its training, would perform an important role in the attack. Some of the division's units would go directly into battle as soon as they arrived in the VIII Corps sector. The green 11th Armored Division would enter into battle alongside the relatively untested 87th Infantry Division. Pictured is the crew of an American M-4 Sherman tank changing the tracks on their vehicle. *National Archives*

extent that it cost him the advantage of the initiative. The German high command evidently considered further extension to the west or north as both logistically and strategically unsound without possession of Bastogne, as the town overlooks the main roads and concentration areas of the spearheads. By the end of the month, the all-out effort in the north had become temporarily defensive; in the west there was a limited withdrawal, and the array of German forces around Bastogne clearly exposed the enemy's anxiety over that position. Until the Bastogne situation is resolved one way or the other, no change in strategy can be expected."

Middleton's VIII Corps was assigned to lead the American attack toward Bastogne. This was to be the American curtain-raiser thrust of the left wing of Patton's Third Army. At Bastogne, it was to pivot on the town and swing northeast to establish contact with the First Army's VII Corps at Houffalize. Successful implementation of this strategy would effectively block the German lines of communication west of Bastogne.

On the evening of December 29 the VIII Corps had taken control of the 101st Airborne Division and the 9th Armored Division. Although General Maxwell Taylor's 101st Airborne Division paratroopers and glider infantry would play no offensive role in the first stages of the Third Army operation, they were ordered to hold the pivot position at Bastogne throughout the entire American offensive operation. Of the 9th Armored commands, only CCA was already committed at the beginning of the VIII Corps advance toward Houffalize. On the morning of December 30, the corps east-to-west order of battle would be the 101st Airborne Division, CCA of the 9th Armored Division, the 11th Armored Division, and the 87th Infantry Division. The 11th Armored and 87th Infantry were designated to make the main effort.

Meanwhile, in the afternoon of December 29, Manteuffel, the German Fifth Panzer Army commander, met with his corps and divisional commanders to inform them of the major attack to begin the next morning. He started the meeting by making some critical remarks about the original failure to appreciate the importance of Bastogne. He then told the assembled officers that the planned Ardennes counteroffensive was at an end. Bastogne had become the "central problem," and the German high command viewed the forthcoming battle as an opportunity to win either a striking victory or to chew up the enemy divisions which would be poured into the coming fight. The planned December 30 operation consisted of three phases: 1) close the ring once again around Bastogne; 2) push the Americans back to the south; 3) with reinforcements now on the way, take Bastogne in a final assault.

At Manteuffel's request, a single commander was placed in charge of all German forces around Bastogne on December 26. The general chosen for the job was General Freiherr V. Luettwitz, formerly in charge of the XLVII Panzer Corps of Manteuffel's Fifth Panzer Army. Army Group Luettwitz, as it was now named, would conduct the fight to restore the German positions around Bastogne using the XXXIX and XLVII Panzer Corps, to attack east to west followed by the second striking west to east.

Since a number of German divisions en route to Bastogne for the attack had not yet arrived, the attack would be neither as strong

The general mission given the 11th Armored Division and the 87th Infantry Division, of Middleton's VIII Corps, was to swing west around Bastogne and capture the heights south of the village of Houffalize, and secure the Ourthe River line. The two-division attack would be supported by 10 battalions of corps artillery. Two Ameican soldiers are seen taking cover at the rear of an M-4 Sherman medium tank. *National Archives*

Across the lines, on the afternoon of December 29, Manteuffel, commander of the Fifth Panzer Army, called his commanders together in conference to inform them that a large-scale attack on Bastogne would take place the next day. The attack would attempt to break the narrow corridor cut into Bastogne by Patton's Fourth Armored Division. Pictured in the Ardennes is a destroyed American towed 3-inch antitank gun. *National Archives*

nor as coordinated as Manteuffel had originally hoped. Due to strong pressure from Hitler for the attack to be launched immediately, Manteuffel was forced to take more risks. The eastern assault force would consist of the 1st SS Panzer and the 167th Volksgrenadier Divisions; its drive was to be made via Lutrebois toward Assenois. From the west of Bastogne, the German forces, led by the Fuehrer Escort Brigade, would aim for the village of Sibret. If the German formations approaching Bastogne from two directions could successfully link up south of the town, they would effectively close the corridor opened by CCR of the Fourth Armored Division on December 26.

The 3d Panzer Grenadier Division was to advance on the left of the Fuehrer Escort Brigade while the battle-scarred remnants of the 26th Volksgrenadier Division and 15th Panzer Grenadier Division advanced to the west and north of Bastogne. The timing for the arrival of the incoming reinforcements from the 12th SS Panzer, the 9th SS Panzer, and the 340th Volksgrenadier Divisions, was unknown.

The eastern attack forces of Army Group Luettwitz managed to capture the village of

Lutrebois (only 1,200 yards from the main Arlon-Bastogne highway) and cut out a salient 4 miles deep and 4 miles wide into the lines of the Third Army's III Corps. The artillery pieces of the Fourth Armored Division poured an unprecedented concentration of rounds into this small area. In the seven days from December 30 to January 6, a total of 24,483 105-millimeter howitzer rounds cascaded into Lutrebios and into the woods north and east of the village. Seven thousand rounds were fired on December 31 alone.

The Germans clung to the Lutrebois pocket for a week, but it cost them dearly. In one day (December 30), they lost 55 tanks to the Fourth Armored Division and 35th Infantry Division, with air support from P-47 Thunderbolts braving a low ceiling.

An extract from the official U.S. Army history of World War describes some of the fighting that took place over the village of Lutrebois on December 30. It begins:

"About 0445 (the hour is uncertain) the enemy started his move toward Lutrebois with tanks and infantry, and at the same time, more infantry crossed the valley and slipped through the lines of the 2nd Battalion. As the first assault force crossed the opening east of Lutrebois, the American cannoneers went into action with such effect as to stop this detachment in its tracks. The next German sortie came in a hook around the north side of Lutrebois. Company L used up all of its bazooka rounds, then was engulfed. The German grenadiers moved on along the western road but were checked there for at least an hour by the heavy machine guns. During this midmorning phase, seven enemy tanks were spotted north of Lutrebois. A platoon of the 654th Tank Destroyer Battalion accounted

Manteuffel's offensive plans for December 30 called for German panzer units to attack the American corridor into Bastogne from two sides. The German attack from the western side of Bastogne never really got started, due to pressure from Patton's VIII Corps. The German attack launched from the eastern side of the American corridor into Bastogne made some limited progress, but was effectively blunted by elements of Patton's III Corps. An American soldier is seen peering into a small Polish-built tracked rmored vehicle pressed into German service. *National Archives*

The exact number of German tanks that took part in Hitler's Ardennes counteroffensive was rounded out by the U.S. Army at 1,800 vehicles. Of that figure, the Americans estimated some 250 were Tiger VI heavy tanks (both the Tiger I and II) and the balance was divided equally between the Mark IV and the Mark V Panther medium tanks. An American soldier is pictured looking over a destroyed Tiger II in the Ardennes. *National Archives*

for four, two were put out of action by artillery high explosive, and one was immobilized by a mine.

"News of the attack reached CCA of the 4th Armored at 0635, and General Earnest promptly turned his command to face east in support of the 35th Division. By 1000 General Dager was reshuffling CCB to take over the CCA positions. The first reinforcement dispatched by CCA was the 51st Armored Infantry Battalion, which hurried in its half-tracks to back up the thin line of the 2nd Battalion. Here, the combination of fog and woods resulted in a very confused fight, but the 2nd Battalion continued to hold in its position while the enemy panzer grenadiers, probably from the 2nd Regiment of the 1st SS Panzer, seeped into the woods to its rear. The headquarters and heavy weapons crews of the 3rd Battalion had meanwhile fallen back to the battalion command post in the Losange Chateau southwest of Lutrebois. There, the 51st Armored Infantry Battalion gave a hand, fighting from half-tracks and spraying the clearing around the Chateau with .50-caliber slugs. After a little of this treatment, the German infantry gave up and retired into the woods.

"During the morning, the advance guard of the 167th Volksgrenadiers, attacking in a column of battalions because of the constricted road net, crossed the Martelange-Bastogne road and reached the edge of the woods southeast of Assenois. Here the grenadiers encountered the 51st. Each German attempt to break into the open was stopped with heavy losses. General Hoecker says the lead battalion was

CLEARING THE BASTOGNE AREA 133

American combat experience in France between June and November 1944 had shown that the various versions of the M-4 Sherman tank was roughly equal to the German Mark IV medium tank. Against the Mark V Panther medium tank, the M-4 Sherman normally won only when it enjoyed numerical superiority. Pictured is the interior of a German Panther tank taken from the rear of the vehicle's turret looking toward the breech end of the vehicle's 75-millimeter high-velocity gun. *British Army Tank Museum*

"cut to pieces" and that the attack by the 167th was brought to naught by the Jabos (fighter-bombers) and the "tree smasher" shells crashing in from the American batteries.

"The main body of the 1st SS Panzer Kampfgruppe (combat group) appeared an hour or so before noon, moving along the Lutremange-Lutrebois road; some 25 tanks were counted in all. It took two hours to bring the fighter-bombers into the fray, but they arrived just in time to cripple or destroy 7 tanks and turn back the bulk of the panzers. Companies I and K still were in their foxholes along the road during the air bombing and would recall that, lacking bazookas, the green soldiers "popped off" at the tanks with their rifles and that some of the German tanks turned aside into the woods. Later the two companies came back across the valley, on orders, and joined the defense line forming near the chateau.

The failure of the Fifth Panzer Army to close the gap opened by Patton's troops at Bastogne convinced General Manteuffel that the time had arrived for the German forces in the Ardennes to relinquish all thought of continuing the offensive. Withdrawal in the west and south to a shortened line was more in keeping with the true combat capability of the gravely weakened German divisions. Visible in this picture are two German armored half-tracks destroyed during the fighting in the Ardennes. *National Archives*

"Thirteen German tanks, which may have debauched (retreated) from the road before the air attack, reached the woods southwest of Lutrebois, but a 4th Armored artillery observer in a cub plane spotted them and dropped a message to Company B of the 35th Tank Battalion. Lt. John A. Kingsley, the company commander, who had six Sherman tanks and a platoon from the 701st Tank Destroyer Battalion, formed an ambush near a slight ridge that provided his own tanks with hull defilade and waited. The leading German company (or platoon), which had six panzers, happened to see Company A of the 35th as the fog lifted, and turned, with flanks exposed, in that direction. The first shot from Kingsley put away the German commander's tank and the other tanks milled about until all had been knocked out. Six more German tanks came along and all were destroyed or disabled. In the meantime, the American tank destroyers took on some accompanying assault guns, shot up three of them and dispersed the neighboring grenadier."

In contrast to the limited success of the German eastern attack force, the western attack forces had barely set out toward Sibret before being repelled. By noon of December 31, Rundstedt's headquarters had agreed that any further attempt to break through the Bastogne corridor via Sibret would depend on the success of the eastern counterattack force, which never materialized.

On December 30, Patton wrote in his notes about the day's events:

"The 11th Armored Division on the right and the 87th Infantry Division on the left jumped off at 0800 and ran into the flank of a German counterattack, headed SE to cut off Bastogne. The German attack consisted of the 130th Panzer Lehr Division and the 26th Volksgrenadier Division. Our attack stopped them and turned them back. At the same time, on the other flank of the Bastogne bulge, the 35th and 26th Infantry Divisions were attacked by the 1st SS Panzer Division and the 167th Volksgrenadier Division. The artillery of the Fourth

The most unusual armored vehicle committed by Hitler to his Ardennes counteroffensive was the massive 70-ton Jagdtiger tank destroyer, armed with a 128-millimeter high-velocity gun. Only 70 were built before the war ended. Pictured is an American soldier inspecting a destroyed Jagdtiger. *National Archives*

CLEARING THE BASTOGNE AREA 135

The counter-battery duels between German and American gunners during the end of December 1944 often forced American gunners to move quickly from one position to another. This was not an easy task, for the artillery carriages quickly froze fast in the terrible cold of an Ardennes winter. It often took blowtorches and crowbars to pry artillery pieces loose so they could be moved to another location. Pictured stuck at the side of an Ardennes road is an American 155-millimeter howitzer and towing tractor. *National Archives*

Armored Division came to the help of the 35th Infantry Division, and the enemy was repulsed with the loss of 55 tanks. This repulse was largely aided by the action of the XIX Tactical Air Command, which was able to fly most of the day despite very bad weather. The 101st Airborne Division also repulsed a counterattack from the NW.

"Unquestionably, this was the critical day of the operation, as there was a concerted effort on the part of the Germans, using at least five divisions, to again isolate Bastogne."

Despite recent events, Patton insisted that III Corps continue its attack toward St. Vith. Millikin, the corps commander, who was being a little bit more cautious than Patton, knew that he would have to alter his plans to reflect the impact of the German attacks of December 30. The original plans had called for the 6th Armored Division from the XII Corps to pass through the Fourth Armored Division (which was now down to only 42 operational tanks), and begin the attack on December 31 with an advance northeast from the Bastogne perimeter. The 35th Infantry Division was to parallel this drive by advancing in the center on a northeast axis, while the 26th Infantry Division, on the III Corps right wing, would turn its attack in a northwesterly direction.

The initial plans for the December 30 offensive had called for the Fourth Armored Division to be passed from Millikin's III Corps to Middleton's VIII Corps, but Middleton agreed that Gaffey's division should continue its support of the hard-pressed 35th Infantry Division. The 26th Infantry Division was now deployed on the north side of the Sure River.

Millikin was keenly aware of the threat presented by the new German offensive operations around Bastogne, but he expected that the attack by the 6th Armored Division (nicknamed the "Super Sixth") would improve the situation. Major General Robert W. Grow, an early supporter of the U.S. Army's tank forces, led the 6th Armored Division into battle. The distance between his XII Corps location and his newly assigned objective was not that great, but Grow knew that the movement would be complicated by the necessity of using a system of roads already suffering gridlock from too many military vehicles.

The attack planned for December 31 by the 6th Armored Division would involve the division's two CCs advancing abreast. CCA, ordered to attack on the right, would use the Arlon-Bastogne highway, while CCB, picked for the left wing, would pass through the VIII Corps area by way of the Neufchâteau-Bastogne road. By daylight of December 31, CCA was in a forward assembly position behind the 101st Airborne line southeast of Bastogne. Due to a series of misunderstandings and mistakes, CCB failed to make its appearance as scheduled.

Colonel Hines, commander of CCA, wanted to postpone his attack until CCB could reach its jumping off location. However, due to a lack of cover combined with heavy enemy fire, Hines and Grow decided to launch a limited objective attack in which the CCA Kennedy and Brown Task Forces would start from a location near the Bastogne-Bras road and thrust northeast. Task Force Kennedy was assigned to capture Neffe and to clear the enemy from the woods to the east. Task Force Brown was assigned to move alongside Task Force Kennedy, scour the woods south of Neffe, and seize the high ground around the village of Wardin on the northeast. The attack, begun shortly after noon, rolled through Neffe with little German opposition. However, a combination of heavy snow squalls and a lack of air support soon slowed CCA's advance to a crawl.

Another problem developed for CCA when the 35th Infantry Division (on its right flank) started to lag behind because of the weather and occasional enemy fire. Just before dark, small German units struck at Hines' exposed flanks, and CCA was forced to stop its advance.

The artillery maintained a protective barrage around CCA throughout the night.

On December 31, Patton wrote in his notes:

"Very bad weather with snow and sleet. Tractors could not be used to tow guns. Necessary to use the diamond-six trucks.

"Germans continued to counterattack strongly, but the 6th Armored Division attacked as planned and made 4 kilometers on its axis. The enemy counterattacked 17 times today—

Despite the large German offensive operation of December 30, there was no thought in the mind of Patton that his III Corps would delay its attack in an northeastern direction toward St. Vith. This advance, set to begin on December 31, would form an important part of the general Third Army offensive begun by Patton's VIII Corps on December 30. Leading the III Corps advance would be the 6th Armored Division. An armored recovery version of the M-4 Sherman tank is pictured here near the ruins of Bastogne. *National Archives*

CLEARING THE BASTOGNE AREA 137

German soldiers feared American artillery much more than they did American tanks. During and after Hitler's Ardennes counteroffensive, German soldiers often described American artillery fire as methodical, schematic, and very wasteful. The last comment reflected the fact that by late 1944, the German war machine was running short of everything. Pictured at the moment of firing is an American 155-millimeter gun, popularly referred to as the "Long Tom." *National Archives*

11 repulsed with heavy losses to the enemy. We also sustained casualties. We lost 9 men killed and 50 wounded. More than 300 German dead counted on the snow.

"Due to severe fighting heretofore sustained, the attack of the 87th Infantry Division and the 17th Airborne Division will be of limited intensity but will retain the initiative."

## The Fighting Continues Into the New Year

On the morning of New Year's Day, 1945, the 6th Armored Division CCB was finally in place on the left of CCA. CCA was to try again to clear the woods and ridges beyond the village of Neffe. CCB was to cut through the German supply routes, feeding into and across the Longvilly road, to permit north-south movement along the eastern face of the Bastogne pocket. This was the same path the Germans were using to assemble their forces near Lutrebois. CCB had divided itself into two task forces to attack Bourcy and Arloncourt, with an eye to the high ground for domination of the German road net.

The commander of CCB was counting on 101st Airborne Division troops on his left flank to push the Germans out of the Bois Jacques north of Bizory. The previous afternoon, Middleton, the VIII Corps commander, had ordered General Maxwell Taylor, commander of the 101st Airborne Division, to use the reserve battalion of the 506th Parachute Infantry for this purpose. He had then countermanded this order. Unfortunately, the 6th Armored Division was unaware of the change in plans until the last minute.

Suddenly lacking the 101st Airborne Division's support and faced with a front normally considered too wide for a linear advance by armor, the commander of the 6th Armored Division put five of its six task forces into the attack on January 2. German resistance to the advance of the division was extreme and even included attacks by the Luftwaffe. Despite heavy losses, the 6th Armored Division had gained much ground by January 2. It would be another eight days before similar gains would be achieved. While the tanks and infantry of the 6th Armored had been effectively supported by artillery throughout the fighting, the division official record gives the main credit for the successes it enjoyed to the fighter-bombers of the XIX Tactical Air Command.

By January 2, the 6th Armored was the only division in Patton's III Corps that had made any progress in the offensive that began on December 30. The 35th Infantry Division, on the right flank of the 6th Armored, had run headlong into the German units battling for Lutrebois and failed to reach its objectives. Even though the German effort to open a path through the left wing of the 35th at

Lutrebois had failed, it had managed to put the 35th out of action. Before the division could regain its place in Patton's offensive operations, it would have to eliminate German opposition at three points: Lutrebois, Villersla-Bonne-Eau, and Harlange.

On December 27, the 26th Infantry Division on the right flank of the 35th Infantry Division had managed to put its leading battalions across the Sure River. Its far-term objective was the village of Wiltz—about four miles to the north of the river. Its near-term objective was the Wiltz-Bastogne highway, then being used by the German Seventh Army to support the build-up of forces east of Bastogne.

At this time, the 80th Infantry Division of the XII Corps was pushing due north and the 26th Infantry Division was pushing northwest. Besieged by its own problems, the 35th Infantry Division was unable to provide the 26th with protection on its left or right flanks. The commander of the 26th Infantry Division was faced with simultaneously leading the III Corps attack while at the same time watching both of his exposed flanks.

## The German View

Brandenberger's Seventh Army became greatly alarmed as the leading battalion of the 26th Infantry Division pushed forward toward Wiltz. Brandenberger saw that the American attacks around Marvie and Harlange could

The effectiveness and accuracy of American artillery fire in the Battle of the Bulge made itself felt throughout most of the fighting. Experienced German artillery officers estimated that their American opponents had an superiority in guns and ammunition of 10 to 1. The crew of an American 105-millimeter howitzer has just fired their weapon. The barrel can be seen in its full recoil position. *National Archives*

The German estimate of the number of artillery pieces employed in the Ardennes by the Americans was far too high. U.S. Army records show that on December 23 there were 4,155 U.S. artillery pieces in the Ardennes, versus roughly 1,000 German artillery pieces. American artillery pieces would eventually fire a total of 1,255,000 rounds at the Germans. Pictured sticking out from its snow-covered firing position is the barrel of an American 105-millimeter howitzer. *National Archives*

suddenly break through and trap the 5th Parachute Division in what the Germans now were calling "the Harlange pocket." The renewal of the 26th Infantry Division attack on January 2 and the threat to the Bastogne-Wiltz road increased the threat to the 5th Parachute Division and the link it provided between the Seventh and Fifth Panzer Army.

Brandenberger asked Model's permission to pull his troops back from Villers-la-Bonne-Eau and Harlange. Manteuffel was also asking permission to withdraw. Model refused both requests, reminding them that Germany now was in a battle of attrition, by which the Allies would become enmeshed and ground down. Model also had no power to order a withdrawal, since Hitler had demanded that the German Army give no ground. It was the Fifth Panzer Army's failure to close the gap around Bastogne that convinced Manteuffel that offensive operations in the Ardennes should be replaced by a withdrawal. Adding to Manteuffel's concern was the capture of the village of Mande-St. Etienne on January 2 by Patton's VIII Corps. With Mande-St. Etienne under Allied control, the three weak German divisions at the tip of the German penetration in the Rochefort area of the Ardennes were in grave danger of being cut off. With permission to withdraw denied, the staff at Army Group B continued to prepare plans for a January 4 offensive to take Bastogne. On January 3, before these desperate plans could be put into effect, the Allies launched another large counteroffensive. This new attack consisted of Patton's Third Army advancing from the south and Hodges' First Army from the north.

In a postwar interview, Manteuffel explained his reactions to this new American counteroffensive:

"An enemy counterattack made on January 3, 1945—and recognized as such—changed events and the conduct of battles at the army front lines completely. I informed the troops of my decision to fall back by fighting delaying actions, stressing the fact that by their mutual cooperation, liaison within the army was to be maintained to prevent a breakthrough by the enemy within the zone of our army. Lack of fuel and the huge lack of recovery and repair services of all kinds forced us to destroy or leave behind considerably more armor than was put out of action by the enemy during the entire attack. In this way artillery too fell into the hands of the enemy without firing.

"Neither Field Marshal Model, nor I, or any other military leader doubted that our forces could no longer resist the enemy pressure. The plan and the suggestion of OB West, Heeresgruppe (Army Group) B and the army had therefore the aim, after a short reorganization of the troops at the starting line of the attack on December 26, to retreat to the Rhine in widespread withdrawal movements. This had been expressively requested several times by Field Marshal Model. Hitler refused to have any discussions whatsoever on this subject."

At the same time that Hitler was refusing to pull the German forces out of the Ardennes, he had already begun to withdraw his Waffen SS divisions, with their duties to be taken over by the Fifth Panzer Army. This was, in effect, Hitler's acknowledgment that the Ardennes

German resistance to the advance of Patton's III Corps was determined and tough. American casualties would soar. Despite the heavy losses incurred, the 6th Armored did make some gains by January 2. A great deal of credit for the division's advance was due to the fighter-bombers of the XIX TAC, which often flew in less than perfect flying conditions. The favorite American ground attack aircraft in Erurope was the rugged Republic P-47 Thumderbolt as pictured. *National Archives*

CLEARING THE BASTOGNE AREA 141

On New Year's Day, the German Luftwaffe launched over 1,000 planes over Holland, Belgium, and Northern France. The intent of this aerial assault was to destroy as many Allied aircraft as possible on the ground. While the Germans did manage to destroy between 300 to 400 Allied aircraft during the attack, they lost over 300 of their own planes and almost as many pilots. Shown in flight is an early model of the German Me-109 fighter plane. *National Archives*

counteroffensive had failed. Manteuffel, extremely upset by this action on Hitler's part, gave this account in a postwar interview:

"A great burden was added to the army when, during the first days of January, orders were given to withdraw the units of the Sixth Panzer Army from the fighting front. The troops and commanders did not comprehend this action, and I protested against it in the sharpest manner. The explanation that these units were wanted for new tasks at the eastern front could not deceive the troops any longer to believe that during these decisive days, once more the Heer (German Army) has to bear the main brunt of the fighting, whereas the units of the Waffen SS first enjoyed what the frontline soldier usually called a 'rest.' The supreme command had once again forgotten to take into account the psychological effects on the troops."

Finally, on January 8, Hitler gave permission for the army units located at the farthest tip of the German penetration in the Ardennes to pull back. A new defensive line was to run generally northeast from Longchamps, toward the eastward bend of the Ourthe River.

## One More Try by Both Sides

On the eve of its new counteroffensive against the German penetration in the Ardennes, the

American First Army consisted of 13 divisions, including three armored, which were divided into three corps. The main thrust of the First Army assault was to be led by Collins' VII Corps. It was to advance southeast between the Ourthe and Lienne Rivers and seize the area around Houffalize. The XVIII Airborne Corps was to advance on the right flank of the VII Corps. The V Corps would hold in place. Elements of two British divisions (in a token display of British involvement) were to push into the German penetration from the west, aiming at an area just short of Houffalize.

Owing to Hitler's preoccupation with taking Bastogne, most of the divisions originally assigned to the Sixth Panzer Army had been shunted southward at the end of December and early in January. At first, the only opposition to the First Army's advance was from three battered enemy divisions, the 12th and 560th Volksgrenadier Divisions, and the 2d SS Panzer Division, supported by the winter weather and the rugged terrain. These influences kept the American advance down to less than a mile a day. Fog deprived the First Army of air support and reduced the effectiveness of its artillery.

On January 13, a CC from the 3rd Armored Division managed to cut off the only major escape route available to the German

The right wing of Patton's III Corps advance consisted of the 26th Infantry Division, which had been brought into line on December 27, when it put it leading battalions across the Sure River. Wiltz, the division objective, was only a little more than four miles to the north. The immediate objective of the division was the Wiltz-Bastogne road. Despite the closeness of its objective, the 26th Infantry Division could make little progress against stiff dug-in German defenses. Pictured along the Wiltz-Bastogne road is a destroyed German Jagdpanzer IV (turretless tank destroyer). *National Archives*

CLEARING THE BASTOGNE AREA   143

Tactically the 26th Infantry Division was on its own in trying to secure the Wiltz-Bastogne road. Due to the rugged Ardennes terrain and stiff German resistance, the American infantry divisions on the 26th flanks were advancing in different directions. Shown is an abandoned German armored half-track tht mounted a 10-tube rocket launcher on its rear deck. *National Archives*

defenders of Houffalize. On the night of January 13, the men of the VII Corps of the First Army could see the lightning-like flashes of artillery pieces supporting Patton's Third Army to the south.

Even though Hitler had begun to withdraw many of his Waffen SS units from the Ardennes, Patton's troops, fighting in the cold biting snow in the Bastogne area on January 3, could see little evidence of German resistance slackening. Every American attempt to move a little farther forward was met by a fierce counterattack, led by one or more German tanks. As with the December 30 offensive by the Third Army, it was the 6th Armored Division on the left wing of the III Corps that made the most progress. On the first day of the renewed offensive, the 6th Armored Division took the battered villages of Oubourcy, Mageret, and Wardin.

On the morning of January 4, the Germans launched their last big offensive aimed at the area around Bastogne. Most of the fighting was centered near the Houffalize highway leading to Bastogne. One of the German objectives turned out to be the village of Longchamps, on the western side of the Houffalize highway, defended by paratroopers of the 101st Airborne Division, part of Patton's VIII Corps.

The first German attack on Longchamps had occurred on January 3—a day earlier than the main attack. It achieved only minor success before being driven off by the American paratroopers. The renewed attack the next day met with even less success. Allied airborne troops claimed 34 German tanks during these two battles.

The German troops on the eastern side of the Houffalize highway, near the eastern end of Bastogne were more successful than their counterparts on the other side of the road. By the end of the day on January 4, the German offensive had recaptured the villages of Oubourcy, Mageret, and Wardin from the 6th Armored Division, although the Germans were unable to make any further progress. The fighting around Bastogne disintegrated into a typical pattern of frequent attacks and counterattacks by both sides. Patton, who was visiting his frontline units on January 4, glumly noted to himself, "We can still lose the war."

The depleted 4th and 6th Armored Divisions had been withdrawn for rest and refitting. However, in reaction to the German offensive of January 4, the commander of Patton's VIII Corps alerted the divisional commanders that they were "on call." Fortunately this drastic action was not needed.

By January 6, Patton began to suspect that the Germans might soon withdraw from their Ardennes positions. Only the day before, Bradley had convinced Patton to transfer a newly available division from the XX Corps to the fighting around the southeast of Bastogne (under III Corps command) rather than to the XII Corps. Patton was not very happy about this turn of events. He had hoped to launch an attack with the XII Corps against the base of the German penetration, and he now worried that the Germans could escape before he could act.

Despite the fact that the Germans had already started to withdraw their armored divisions from the Ardennes by January 3, Patton's Third Army troops around Bastogne saw

The 6th Armored Division advance was just getting under way on January 1, and the 35th Infantry Division's advance was already stalled by strong German resistance. The commander of Patton's III Corps gave orders on January 2 for the 26th Infantry Division to renew its efforts to cut the Wiltz-Bastogne road, which was supporting not only the German Seventh Army but a portion of the enemy build-up east of Bastogne. In the Ardennes sits an abandoned German armored recovery vehicle, based on the chassis of the Panther medium tank. *National Archives*

CLEARING THE BASTOGNE AREA 145

The commander of the 26th Infantry Division redoubled his efforts to secure the Wiltz-Bastogne road, but to no avail. However, the new attacks by the American infantry division did manage to unnerve the German commander of the Seventh Army, who feared that he would be cut off from the Fifth Panzer Army. He therefore asked his superiors for permission to withdraw and was refused. American infantrymen in snowsuits are pictured heading into battle. *National Archives*

no evidence of a German withdrawal as late as January 8. Surveillance patrols around Bastogne found the Germans as full of fight as ever.

On January 9, the III Corps, having reorganized itself from the blows it suffered from the German offensive launched on January 4, rejoined the general Third Army offensive operations. On January 9 Patton wrote in his notes:

"Limited flying weather. The attack of the VIII and III Corps jumped off as planned. The 90th Infantry Division, making the main effort, received heavy casualties from artillery and rocket fire just after the jump-off, but advanced two kilometers. The 101st Airborne and Fourth Armored Divisions moved forward, the former securing the woods west of Noville. The remaining units in the two corps made very limited progress."

On January 10 Patton wrote:

"Higher authority decided that an armored division (Fourth Armored Division) should be withdrawn from the line as a precautionary measure against the possible German attack from Saarbrucken (located to the southeast of the Ardennes in the sector assigned to Patton's XX Corps).

"The attack of the 101st Airborne and Fourth Armored Divisions was therefore called off at noon, and the 4th Armored will withdraw during darkness. At the same time, the 101st Airborne Division and the 6th Armored Division will link up. The entire VIII Corps will limit offensive operations to vigorous patrolling. III Corps continues attack. All the arrangements for this change were made by personal contact between the army commander and corps and divisions involved.

By January 3 what remained of the German forces within the Ardennes had exhausted their potential for large-scale offensive actions. They would now be on the defensive, trying only to defend the gains already achieved. German prisoners are seen being escorted into the POW holding area. *National Archives*

One day after Hodges' First Army began its attack from the northern flank of the German penetration, Patton's Third Army, which had been attacking in the Ardennes since December 22, started a new phase in its campaign to push in the southern flank of the German penetration in the Ardennes. Two American soldiers are seen looking over a destroyed German Mark IV medium tank in the Ardennes. *National Archives*

"All elements of the III Corps, particularly the 90th Infantry Division, made fair progress. A column of German guns and armor, attempting to withdraw in front of the 90th Infantry Division, was brought under artillery fire and also attacked by fighter-bombers from the XIX Tactical Air Command with good results.

"General Bradley secured authority to advance the 9th Armored and 8th Armored Divisions, now on the Meuse, to the Moselle between Pont A Mousson and Thionville. This, with the presence of the Fourth Armored Division south of Luxembourg, makes the situation, so far as a German attack from Saarbrucken is concerned, very satisfactory."

It was not until January 11 that Third Army reports reflected firm indications of a German withdrawal in the Ardennes. From that point on the Germans steadily began to give up ground. This was reflected in Patton's notes beginning on January 11: "III Corps making fair progress and securing a larger number of prisoners." On January 12 Patton wrote: "The VIII Corps resumes attack on Houffalize as follows from west to east: 87th Infantry, 17th Airborne, 11th Armored, and 101st Airborne Divisions. The III Corps continues attack for the final mopping up of the salient, SE of Bastogne."

From January 11 forward, as German resistance continued to crumble in the face of the Third Army's advance, the belief that the Battle of the Bulge was nearing its end raised the morale of Patton's troops. Patton took notice of this fact in his notes of January 13:

"Attitude of troops completely changes.

They now have full confidence that they are pursuing a defeated enemy. This in spite of the fact that the Germans north and northeast of Bastogne are resisting viciously in order to preserve their escape routes."

On January 12 the Soviet army launched its massive winter offensive from the frozen plains of southern Poland, and quickly began to punch holes in the German defensive lines. As early as December 20, Eisenhower had urged the Russians to begin their winter offensive to help relieve the pressure on his armies in the Ardennes. Fully aware of the threat of this new Soviet offensive, Hitler quickly began to move units out of the Ardennes toward the eastern front. The eastern front had not received any significant reinforcements since Hitler had begun preparations for his Ardennes counteroffensive.

On January 14, Rundstedt appealed to Hitler to authorize a further withdrawal in the Ardennes. The line Hitler earlier had picked west of Houffalize was already compromised in the north and was being rolled up in the south. Rundstedt asked approval to pull back farther to anchor a new defensive line on the high ground just east of Houffalize so that it extended northward behind the Salm River and southward through existing positions east of Bastogne.

Having accepted by this point in time that his grand Ardennes counteroffensive was finished, Hitler gave Rundstedt permission to form a new defensive line as he had suggested. Stubborn to the end, Hitler still refused Rundstedt's and Model's pleas to withdraw all German troops from the Ardennes. Hitler informed Rundstedt and Model that they could withdraw only by fighting their way back to the Siegfried Line.

An extract from a German newspaper article dated January 14, 1945 reflects the

When the American First and Third Armies began to attack the German penetration in the Ardennes on January 3, 1945, the Allied armies were at a peak strength of 3,724,927 men. Those men were divided into three army groups, which in turn were divided into nine field armies (including one not yet assigned any divisions). A column of American M-36 tank destroyers is traveling down a fog-shrouded Ardennes road. *National Archives*

The nine field armies under Eisenhower's command in Europe on January 3, 1945, contained 20 corps. Within these 20 corps were a total of 73 divisions. Of those divisions, 49 were infantry, 20 armored, and four airborne. Seen in this group photo from left to right are Bradley, Major General Leonard T. Gerow of the V Corps, Eisenhower, and Major General J. Lawton Collins, VII Corps commander. *National Archives*

semiofficial summary of Hitler's Ardennes counteroffensive. It begins:

"Four weeks have gone by since von Rundstedt's powerful offensive thrust against the Luxembourg-Belgian area crushed this sector of the American front. The effects resembled those of a double blow to right and left which caused leaks, so to speak, in the Aachen and Saar regions, thereby compelling the energies stored up there for major operations to flow off and exhaust themselves in another direction. This direction, from the point of view of the enemy, was contrary to his interests and was operationally useless. From the military viewpoint, the most important fact, and one which is openly admitted by the enemy, is that because of the number of men and quantity of material lost in this winter operation, their operational plans must be postponed."

On January 15, a patrol from the 101st Airborne Division (part of Patton's VIII Corps) entered the village of Noville, 5 miles south of Houffalize. Early the next morning, the 11th Armored, also part of the VIII Corps, secured the high ground immediately south of Houffalize. Shortly afterward, a patrol from the 11th Armored Division met a patrol from the 2nd Armored Division, belonging to the First Army's VII Corps, outside the town. Patton's notes of January 16 describe the meeting:

"At 0905, 41st Cavalry of the 11th Armored Division made contact with 41st Infantry of the 2nd Armored Division in Houffalize, thus

150  PATTON AND THE BATTLE OF THE BULGE

terminating the Bastogne operation so far as the Third Army is concerned."

This meeting at the shoulders of the German penetration was somewhat of an empty accomplishment, since the slow pace of the American advance had allowed most of the best German units within the Ardennes to escape to fight another day. Patton had foreseen this situation from the beginning, but had not been successful in persuading his superiors to prevent it.

Patton now knew that he could not stage a large attack northward across the German frontier to Prum to prevent the remaining Germans from retreating behind the Siegfried Line. Eisenhower and Montgomery planned for the Third Army to continue attacking northward in the direction of St. Vith. Once this objective was achieved, the mop-up of remaining German forces in the eastern half of the Ardennes would begin.

Bradley, who was now in command of Hodges' First Army again, proposed that once the First Army took St. Vith, Hodges could send a corps to link up with the XII Corps of Patton's Third Army, to form a shallow envelopment for trapping any German forces still within the Ardennes. This plan was ultimately rejected. Instead, the First and Third Armies advanced in a methodical manner in an eastern direction, slowly pushing back the rear guard formations left by the Germans. It would take until the end of January before the two American armies reached the German frontier and reestablished the line that had existed prior to Hitler's launching of his Ardennes counteroffensive.

In a postwar interview with his Allied captors, Manteuffel, the Fifth Panzer Army commander, described his feelings regarding the value of Hitler's Ardennes counteroffensive:

"The fortress of Germany got a breathing spell. The home front, which had been attacked constantly by the enemy air forces, was relieved for a while. However, sacrifices and costs, it is true, were so large that it seems doubtful

Aerial support for Eisenhower's ground forces in early January 1945 came from six tactical air commands (TACs). The Allied TAC operations in the Ardennes fighting was mainly directed against tanks, trucks, and large troop concentrations. Hitler had high hopes of employing newly built jets like the Me-262 fighter, as pictured, to even the odds in the air against the Allies. As with so many others of Hitler's so-called "wonder weapons" the Me-262 was a case of too few too late. *National Archives*

CLEARING THE BASTOGNE AREA 151

In total, the various American and British TACs that flew over the Ardennes in December 1944 and January 1945 claimed to have destroyed 413 enemy armored vehicles. Later ground inspections set the number of kills inflicted by air attack at about 1/10 the number claimed by the Allied ground attack pilots. Two American soldiers are seen examining the destroyed remains of a German StuG III assault gun that had its onboard ammunition explode as evident by the amount of damage to the vehicle. *National Archives*

whether the offensive was really a gain. The last German reserves were badly damaged, they were lacking in effectiveness for continuation of the war in the West as well as the East. The quick success of the Red Army stood in causal

In the main, it fell to the infantrymen of the First Army to push toward the objective, the village of Houffalize. It would take the First Army until January 13 just to reach the area around the town. It was at Houffalize that the First Army was to link up with the VIII Corps of Patton's Third Army, coming up from the south. American soldiers in snowsuit are pictured dashing through the trees of an Ardennes forest. *National Archives*

coherence with the offensive in the Ardennes, which possibly accelerated the end of the war, in which case the gaining of time in the West must be regarded as a false conclusion. The reaction on the morale and in consequence upon the total attitude of the troops and the nation probably accelerated the breakdown of the armed forces and the country."

An American soldier writing in the May 1945 issue of "Infantry Journal," reprinted with permission of the Association of the U.S. Army (AUSA), summed up the fighting in the Ardennes from the viewpoint of an enlisted man. It read:

"The Battle of the Bulge was one of the hardest, if not the hardest, fight of the Allied armies in Europe. The weather, the terrain, and the enemy combined to make a campaign of peculiar bitterness and difficulty.

"The Germans did not try to hold an organized line. They aimed at delaying us to cover

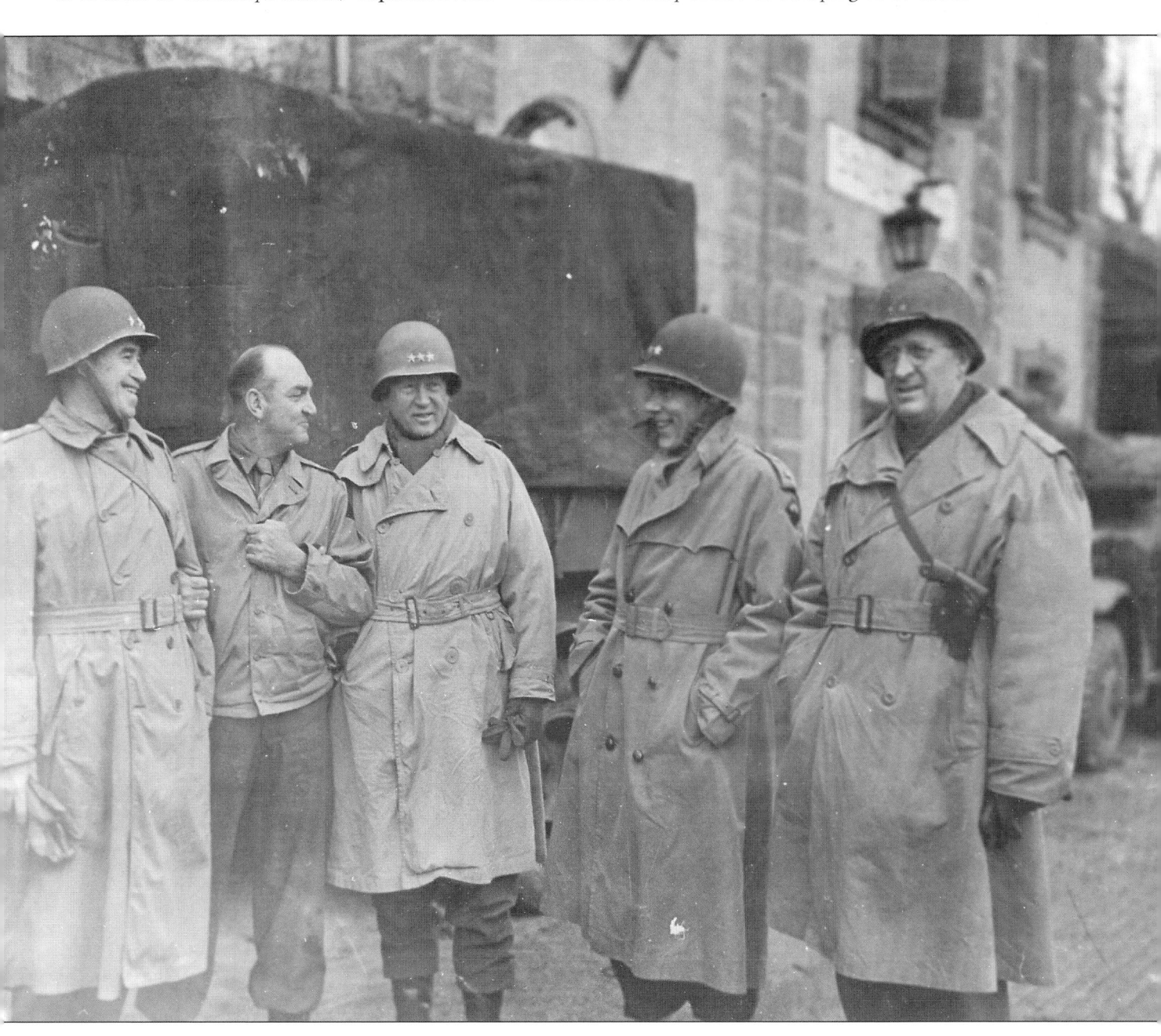

As Patton's Third Army prepared to renew its efforts on January 4 to clear the entire area around Bastogne, it was faced with the largest concentration of German troops (nine divisions) remaining in the Ardennes. Seen in this picture are Bradley on the far left, Patton in the center, and Middleton, the VIII commander, on the far right. *Real War Photos*

154　Patton and the Battle of the Bulge

On January 4 the Germans launched another series of attacks around Bastogne that managed to blunt the advance of Patton's Third Army. As the two sides struggled in the fierce Ardennes winter, neither Patton nor his troops could see any end to the bloody fighting. Visible in this picture are from left to right an M-36 tank destroyer, an M-4 Sherman tank with a short-barrel 75-millimeter gun, and on the far right an M-4 Sherman tank with a long-barrel 76-millimeter gun. *National Archives*

The German Fifth Panzer Army knew that it needed complete control of the Bastogne road net to secure its southern flank against Patton's Third Army. This in turn would allow it to provide additional support to help the Sixth Panzer Army resist the American First Army offensive coming down from the north. Sitting in the middle of an Ardennes town is an abandoned German Panther medium tank. *National Archives*

their own withdrawal. They tried to hold hills, villages, roads, and woods with relatively small delaying parties, supported by mobile guns. They did not make a gesture of holding. They held tenaciously and gave way only when we pushed the attack even more tenaciously. On the whole, their performance was skillful and stubborn, but only a terrain almost ideal to defend in made such a strategy possible. If the enemy was finally forced back, by far the largest credit must go to the men who shouldered rifles and carried machine guns and mortars in freezing weather, plunged through knee-deep and waist-high snow, dug foxholes in ground as hard as steel, stormed hill after hill in the face of perfect enemy observation, and cleaned out woods as dark as night in the middle of the day.

On January 16 elements of Patton's VIII Corps linked up with elements of Hodges First Army at Houffalize. Due to the Soviet advances, Hitler ordered what was left of the Sixth Panzer Army, as well as other supporting units, sent to the eastern front on January 22. *National Archives*

It would take until January 11 before the Third Army would see any slacking in the German will to resist. The American cause in the Ardennes would now be aided by a massive Soviet offensive on the eastern front that began the next day. Visible is the top half of a German soldier who died in the Ardennes fighting. *National Archives*

# Selected Bibliography

Allen, Robert S. *Patton's Third U.S. Army: Lucky Forward*. New York: Manor Books, 1974.

Blumenson, Martin. *Breakout and Pursuit*. United States Army in World War II. Washington, D.C.: U.S. Army, Office of the Chief of Military History, 1961.

Blumenson, Martin. *The Patton Papers*, 2 vols. Houghton Mifflin, 1974.

Bradley, Omar N. *A Soldier's Story*. New York: Rand McNally, 1951; reprint ed., New York: Rand McNally, 1978.

Cole, Hugh M. *The Ardennes: The Battle of the Bulge*. U.S. Army in World War II. Washington, D.C.: U.S. Army, Office of the Chief of Military History, 1965.

Cole, Hugh M. *The Lorraine Campaign*. United States Army in World War II. Washington, D.C.: U.S. Army, Office of the Chief of Military History, 1950.

D' Este, Carlo. *Patton: A Genius For War*. New York: Harper Collins Publishers, Inc. 1995.

Ellis, John. *The Sharp End: The Fighting Man in World War II*. New York: Charles Scribner's Sons, 1980.

Essame, H. *Patton :A Study In Command*. New York: Charles Scribner' s Sons. 1974.

Forty, George. *U.S. Army Handbook,* Ian Allan Ltd.,1979.

Forty, George. *The Armies of George S. Patton*. London: Arms and Armour Press, 1996.

Greenfield, Kent R.; Palmer, Robert R.; and Wiley, Bell I. *The Organization of Ground Combat Troops*. United States Army in World War II. Washington, D.C.: U.S. Army, Office of the Chief of Military History, 1947.

Harrison, Gordon A. *Cross-Channel Attack*. United States Army in World War II. Washington, D.C.: U.S. Army, Office of the Chief of Military History, 1950.

Hastings, Max. *Overload: D-Day and the Battle for Normandy*. London: Pan Books Ltd., 1985.

Irving, David. *The War Between the Generals: Inside the Allied High Command*. New York: Congdon & Lattes, Inc., 1981.

MacDonald, Charles B. *The Last Offensive*. United States Army in World War II. Washington, D.C.: U.S. Army, Office of the Chief of Military History, 1973.

MacDonald, Charles B. *The Siegfried Line Campaign*. United States Army in World War II. Washington, D.C.: U.S. Army, Office of the Chief of Military History, 1950.

Palmer, Robert R.; Wiley, Bell I.; and Keast, William R. *The Army Ground Forces: The Procurement and Training of Ground Combat Troops*. United States Army in World War II. Washington, D.C.: U.S. Army, Office of the Chief of Military History, 1948.

Patton, George S., Jr. *War as I Knew It*. Boston: Houghton Mifflin, 1947; reprint ed., New York: Bantam Books, 1981.

Pogue, Forest C. *The Supreme Command*. United States Army in World War II. Washington, D.C.: U.S. Army, Office of the Chief of Military History, 1954.

Province, Charles M. *The Unknown Patton*. New York: Hippocrence, 1983.

Province, Charles M. *Patton's Third Army*. New York: Hippocrence, 1991.

Province, Charles M. *Patton's One-Minute Messages*. Novato CA: Presidio Press, 1995.

Weigley, Russell. *Eisenhower's Lieutenants*. Bloomington: Indiana University Press, 1981.

Whiting, Charles. *Patton*. New York: Ballantine Books, 1970.

Wilmot, Chester. *The Struggle For Europe*. New York: Carroll & Graf Publishers, Inc. 1986.

# Index

1st Battalion, 318th Infantry (U.S.), 99, 116
1st SS Panzer Corps (Germany), 49, 131, 133-135
2nd Armored Division (U.S), 150
2nd Battalion, 318th Infantry (U.S.), 99, 100
2nd SS Panzer Division (Germany), 52, 143
3rd Armored Division (U.S.), 143
3rd Panzergrenadier Division (Germany), 81, 126, 131
4th Infantry Division (U.S.), 79, 83, 145
41st Infantry Division (U.S.), 150
5th Infantry Division (U.S.), 79
5th Parachute Division (Germany), 60, 83, 86, 88, 90, 93, 140
6th Armored Division (U.S.), 64, 79, 80, 97, 114, 122, 136, 138, 144, 145, 147
6th Army Group (U.S.), 16, 18, 24, 72, 122
8th Armored Division (U.S.), 148
9th Armored Division (U.S.), 57, 63, 79, 83, 129, 148
9th SS Panzer Division (Germany), 81, 131
10th Armored Division (U.S.), 65, 79, 83, 97
11th Armored Division (U.S.), 9, 114, 123, 127-129, 135, 148, 150
12th Army Group (U.S.), 14, 18, 32, 33, 38, 64, 78, 83, 123, 127
12th SS Panzer Division (Germany), 131
12th Volksgrenadier Division (Germany), 143
15th Panzergrenadier Division (Germany), 81, 131
17th Airborne Division (U.S.), 114, 127, 148
21st Army Group (U.S.), 9, 12, 18, 26, 32, 36-38, 43, 78, 82
22nd Armored Artillery Battalions (U.S.), 107
26th Infantry Division (U.S.), 64, 79, 80, 83, 85, 87, 91, 97, 135, 136, 139, 140, 143, 144
26th Volksgrenadier Division (Germany), 52, 53, 77, 80, 89, 131, 135
28th Infantry Division (U.S.), 79
35th Battalion (U.S.), 57
35th Infantry Division (U.S.), 79, 80, 97, 98, 132, 135, 136-139
37th Tank Battalion (U.S.), 91, 101, 105, 106, 135
42nd Infantry Division (U.S.), 79
44th Battalion (U.S.), 57
53rd Armored Infantry Battalion (U.S.), 91, 101, 103, 105
66th Armored Artillery Battalion (U.S.), 107
80th Infantry Division (U.S.), 79, 84, 85, 97, 114, 139
82nd Airborne Division (U.S.), 71
87th Infantry Division (U.S.), 79, 114, 123, 127-129, 135, 148
90th Infantry Division (U.S.), 79, 147, 148
94th Armored Artillery Battalions (U.S.), 107
94th Armored Field Artillery Battalion (U.S.), 101
95th Infantry Division (U.S.), 79
101st Airborne Division (U.S.), 61, 63, 64, 67, 71, 77, 79-81, 90, 102, 110, 116, 117, 129, 136, 144, 147, 148, 150
106th Infantry Division (U.S.), 79
130th Panzer Lehr Division (Germany), 135
150th Battalion (U.S.), 57
167th Volksgrenadier Division (Germany), 131, 133, 135
168th Battalion (U.S.), 57
177th Field Artillery Battalion (U.S.), 101

212th Volksgrenadier Division (Germany), 59, 86
276th Volksgrenadier Division (Germany), 59, 86
318th Infantry (U.S.), 99, 113
325th Volksgrenadier Division (Germany), 83
340th Volksgrenadier Division (Germany), 59, 131
352nd Volksgrenadier Division (Germany), 59, 60, 86
501st Airborne Infantry (Germany), 81
506th Parachute Infantry (U.S), 138
560th Volksgrenadier Division (Germany), 143
600th Army Engineer Battalion (Germany), 52
705th Tank Destroyer Battalion (U.S.), 64, 83

Advanced Echelon 80th Division, 83
Ardennes, 7, 9, 26, 27, 32, 35, 45, 46, 48, 49, 51-53, 55-57, 59-63, 71, 78, 80, 82, 133, 141, 151
Army Group B (Germany), 47, 48, 140
Army Group Luettwitz, 130
British Corps, 31
Combat Command A, 51st Armored Infantry Battalion (U.S.), 99
Combat Command A, 6th Armored Division (U.S), 136, 137
Combat Command A, 9th Armored Division (U.S.), 110, 114, 116, 124, 126, 129
Combat Command A, Fourth Armored Division (U.S.), 87-91, 97, 98, 100, 104, 117-119, 133
Combat Command B, 10th Armored Division (U.S.), 64, 80, 81
Combat Command B, 11th Armored Division (U.S.), 126
Combat Command B, 6th Armored Division (U.S.), 136
Combat Command B, 7th Armored Division (U.S.), 57
Combat Command B, Fourth Armored Division (U.S.), 87-89, 91, 97, 98, 100, 102, 104, 105, 112, 117-119, 133
Combat Command Reserve, 9th Armored Division (U.S.), 80
Combat Command Reserve, Fourth Armored Division (U.S.), 91, 93, 97, 98, 100-103, 105, 111-116, 118, 124, 131
Fifth Panzer Army, 51, 53, 55, 56, 59, 60, 62, 78, 80, 81, 98, 115, 134, 140, 141, 155
First Airborne Division (England), 14
First Allied Airborne Army, 12
First Army (Canada), 12, 31, 38
First Army (France), 24, 35
First Army (U.S.), 14, 26, 34-36, 38, 43, 63, 64, 78, 122, 140, 144, 151, 152, 156
Fourth Armored Division, 54, 79, 82-85, 90, 91, 93, 97, 100, 102, 104, 110, 113, 116, 132, 136, 147
Fueher Escort Brigade, 126, 131
III Corps (U.S.), 64, 65, 79, 80, 82, 83, 85, 86, 89, 91, 93, 97, 98, 103, 116, 118, 120, 122, 127, 132, 136, 144, 147, 148
LIII Corps (Germany), 59
Luftwaffe, 10, 40, 59, 142
LVIII Corps (Germany), 52, 56
LXVI Corps (Germany), 52, 56
LXVII Corps (Germany), 49
LXXX Corps (Germany), 59, 60
LXXXV Corps (Germany), 59

Ninth Air Force, 22
Ninth Army (U.S.), 64, 78
Operation Cobra, 84
Operation Market Garden, 12, 14, 36, 38
Panzer Lehr Division, 45, 52, 53, 80, 81
Red Ball Express, 22, 34
Rundstedt Offensive, 48
Second Army (England), 12, 36
Second Army (U.S.), 14
Seventh Army (Germany), 59, 60, 62, 86, 116, 139
Seventh Army (U.S.), 24, 79, 80, 140
Seventh Panzer Army, 49
Siegfried Line, 8, 28, 33, 36-38, 122, 149, 151
Sixth Panzer Army, 9, 43, 49, 51, 53, 55, 142, 143, 155, 156
Soviet Summer Offensive, 8
Task Force Arloncourt, 138
Task Force Bourcy, 138
Task Force Brown, 136
Task Force Collins, 124-126
Task Force Ezell, 92
Task Force Karsteter, 124-126
Task Force Kennedy, 136
Task Force Pat, 126
Task Force Poker, 126, 127
Task Force Polk, 80
Third Reich, 40
Volksgrenadier Divisions, 68

V Corps (U.S.), 14, 36, 143
VII Corps (U.S.), 14, 25, 53, 55, 67, 71, 79, 129, 143, 144, 150
VIII Corps (U.S.), 36, 56, 57, 62, 63, 65, 77, 78, 80, 122-125, 128, 129, 136, 140, 144, 145, 147, 148, 150, 152, 156
XII Corps (U.S.), 25, 36, 80, 83, 85, 97, 98, 122, 123, 136, 139, 145, 151
XIX Corps (U.S.), 14
XIX Tactical Air Command (TAC), 78, 79, 89, 104, 112, 118, 136, 138, 148
XLVII Panzer Corps, 47, 51, 52, 56, 77, 78, 80, 115, 130
XV Corps (U.S.), 36, 80
XVIII Airborne Corps (U.S.), 143
XX Corps (U.S.), 25, 36, 67, 79, 97, 145
XXI Corps (U.S.), 79
XXXIX Panzer Corps, 130

Abrams, Lieutenant Colonel Creighton W., 101, 103, 105
Baade, Major General Paul W., 98
Beyer, Generalder Infanterie Franz
Blanchard, Colonel, 102
Boggess, First Lieutenant Charles Jr., 106, 107, 109
Bradley, Lieutenant General Omar N., 14, 20, 22, 32, 35, 36, 55, 61, 63-65, 67, 78, 82, 84, 122, 145, 148, 150, 151, 153
Brandenberger, General der Panzertruppen Erich, 59, 60, 62, 98, 140
Brereton, Lieutenant General Lewis H., 12
Clark, Brigadier General Bruce C., 57

Codman, Colonel Charles R., 77
Collins, Lieutenant General J. Lawton, 120, 150
Connaughton, Major George W., 98
Dager, Brigadier General Holmes, 88
Dempsy, Lieutenant General Sir Miles C., 12
Devers, General Jacob L., 16, 24
Dickerman, Corporal Milton, 107
Dietrich, General Joseph "Sepp", 43, 49, 51, 59
Eddy, Major General Manton S., 123
Eisenhower, General Dwight D., 9-12, 15, 16, 18, 20, 22, 32, 33, 35-39, 55, 61, 63, 64, 71, 72, 75, 78, 82, 84, 120-122, 149, 150, 151
Gaffey, Major General Hugh J., 84, 95, 97, 98, 136
Gardner, Lieutenant Colonel Glenn H., 99
Gay, General Hobart R., 65
Gerow, Major General Leonard T., 150
Goebbels, Joseph, 13, 14
Grow, Major General Robert W., 136
Harrold, Colonel Thomas L., 124
Hendrix, Private James, 107-109
Himmler, Heinrich, 13, 14
Hines, Colonel, 136
Hodges, Lieutenant General Courtney H., 14, 22, 35, 38, 82
Jaques, Lieutenant Colonel George, 101, 105
Jodl, General Alfred, 40
Kingsley, Lieutenant John A., 135
Kneiss, General Bapist, 59
Koch, Colonel Oscar W., 64
Kokott, Generalleutnant Heinz, 52
Luettwitz, General der Panzertruppen Heinrich von, 47, 52, 53, 80, 81, 130
Maddox, Colonel Halley G., 65
Manteuffel, Lieutenant General Baron Hasso-Eccard von, 51-53, 56, 59, 60, 80, 92, 130, 131, 134, 140, 142, 151
Marshall, General George C., 25
McAuliffe, Brigadier General Anthony C., 69, 71, 81, 90, 115, 117
Middleton, Major General Troy, 25, 36, 53, 55, 63, 82, 107, 124, 136, 138, 153
Millikin, Major General John, 82, 95, 97, 136
Model, Field Marshal Wolther, 47, 48, 51, 140, 141, 149
Montgomery, Field Marshal Bernard, 9, 15, 30, 32, 36-39, 78, 122, 151
Murphy, Private James, 107
Roosevelt, Franklin D., 44
Rundstedt, Field Marshal Gerd von, 45, 47, 48, 53, 149
Schelde Estuary, 9, 12, 16, 32, 39
Simpson, Lieutenant General William H., 36, 82, 123
Smith, Private Hubert, 107
Stimson, Henry L., 25, 28, 29
Strong, Major General Ken, 63, 64
Taylor, Major General Maxwell D., 71, 117, 138
Vanderberg, Major General Hoyt, 22, 35
Weyland, General Otto P., 69